THE MEN
WILL TALK
TO ME

WEST CORK INTERVIEWS
BY ERNIE O'MALLEY

A page from the Maurice 'Mossy' Donegan interview.
(UCDA O'Malley Notebooks P17b/108, p. 73. *Courtesy of UCD Archives.*)

THE MEN WILL TALK TO ME

West Cork Interviews by Ernie O'Malley

Edited by
Andy Bielenberg, John Borgonovo and Pádraig Óg Ó Ruairc

Preface by
Cormac K. H. O'Malley

MERCIER PRESS
Irish Publisher – Irish Story

MERCIER PRESS
Cork
www.mercierpress.ie

© Original notebooks of Ernie O'Malley, UCD Archives
© Preface: Cormac K. H. O'Malley, 2015
© Introduction and footnotes: Andy Bielenberg, John Borgonovo and Pádraig Óg Ó Ruairc, 2015

ISBN: 978 1 78117 246 9

10 9 8 7 6 5 4 3 2 1

A CIP record for this title is available from the British Library

Printed and bound in the EU.

CONTENTS

To Tomás Ó Ruairc

Acknowledgements

Numerous people helped make this book possible. We would like to thank Mercier Press for its commitment to publishing the Ernie O'Malley interviews in the series *The Men Will Talk to Me*. Mary Feehan has championed this important primary source material, which Mercier is making available to historians, researchers, students and the general public. She and her team deserve high praise for delivering these volumes.

Cormac O'Malley has also been a driving force behind *The Men Will Talk to Me* project. His passion and commitment to the Ernie O'Malley historical record have inspired numerous historians to engage in the arduous transcription process. Cormac also made a number of fascinating contributions to the 2014 Ernie O'Malley Symposium, held at New York University. He, Professor Joe Lee, Dr Nick Wolfe, and the other event organisers at the Glucksman Ireland House should be thanked for putting on that outstanding event, which has contributed to rectifying the long-standing academic neglect of Ernie O'Malley. It also helped to inform aspects of this volume.

Our transcription process benefited from the generous assistance of Seamus Helferty and his staff at the University College Dublin Archives, where the original transcripts are kept. We would like to recognise the assistance kindly provided by Dr Cornelius Buttimer and Professor Emeritus Seán Ó Coileán of the Department of Modern Irish at University College Cork in providing Irish language translations for specific sections of the text. Dr Tim Horgan of Tralee also made his extensive expertise on Ernie O'Malley available to us. Additional assistance came from Dan Breen of the Cork Public Museum, Brian McGee of the Cork City and County Archives, and the staff at the Local Studies Department in the Cork City Library.

Historian Ted O'Sullivan, whose grandfather's testimony appears in this volume, generously offered us relevant historical documents, photographs and information. We would also like to thank Diarmuid Begley and Barbara O'Driscoll, for their assistance. Finally, thanks to Dr Linda Connolly and Anne-Maria McCarthy for their continued support.

The Editors

ABBREVIATIONS

AOH	Ancient Order of Hibernians
Auxie/Auxies	Auxiliary Division of the RIC
BMH	Bureau of Military History
CID	Criminal Investigation Department
EOM	Ernie O'Malley
GAA	Gaelic Athletic Association
GHQ	General Headquarters
GOC	General Officer Commanding
IRA	Irish Republican Army
IRB	Irish Republican Brotherhood
The Joy	Mountjoy Gaol, Dublin
Lt	Lieutenant
NCO	Non-Commissioned Officer
O/C	Officer Commanding
PA	Póilíní Airm (military police)
RIC	Royal Irish Constabulary
TD	Teachta Dála
Tintown	Tintown Internment Camps (in the Curragh)
UCDA	University College Dublin Archives
V/C	Vice-Commanding Officer
WS	Witness Statement

PREFACE

INTRODUCING THE ERNIE O'MALLEY MILITARY INTERVIEWS

CORMAC K. H. O'MALLEY

Though born in Castlebar, County Mayo, in 1897, Ernie O'Malley moved to Dublin with his family in 1906 and attended CBS secondary school and university there. After the 1916 Rising he joined the Irish Volunteers while pursuing his medical studies, but in early 1918 he left home and went on the run. He rose through the ranks of the Volunteers and later the Irish Republican Army, and by the time of the Truce in July 1921 at the end of the War of Independence, or Tan War as it was known to him, he was commandant-general of the 2nd Southern Division, covering parts of Limerick, Tipperary and Kilkenny, with over 7,000 men under his command.

O'Malley was suspicious of a compromise being made during the peace negotiations which resulted in the Anglo-Irish Treaty of December 1921 and reacted strongly against the Treaty when it was announced. As the split developed in the senior ranks of the IRA in early 1922, he was appointed director of organisation for the anti-Treaty Republicans, who then took over the Four Courts in April. When the Four Courts garrison surrendered in June, he managed to escape immediately and was promoted to acting assistant chief of staff and officer commanding the Northern and Eastern Divisions, or half of Ireland. In early November he was captured in a dramatic shoot-out and was severely wounded. Ironically his wounds probably saved his life, as otherwise he would have been court-martialled and executed. While in Mountjoy Gaol in 1923, O'Malley was elected as TD for North Dublin and later, despite his poor health, he joined the forty-one-day hunger strike. Nevertheless, he survived – a matter of mind over body!

Having been released from prison in July 1924 and still in poor health, O'Malley went to the south of Europe to help recover his health. He returned to his medical studies in 1926, but in 1928 headed for the United States. While there he wrote his much acclaimed autobiographical memoir, *On Another Man's Wound*. It was published in 1936, after he had returned to Dublin in 1935. He had spent seven years writing that book, which he meant to be more of a generic story of the Irish struggle than of his own activities. The book was a literary success and added to his reputation among his former comrades.

O'Malley's memoir on the Civil War was not ready for publication, as it required more research, and over the next twenty years he sought to become more familiar with the Civil War period as a whole. What started out in the late 1930s as an effort to supplement his own lack of knowledge, had developed by 1948 into a full-blown enterprise to record the voices, mostly Republican, of his comrades of the 1916–23 struggle for independence. He interviewed more than 450 survivors, across a broad spectrum of people, covering the Tan War and the Civil War – all this at a time when the government was establishing the Bureau of Military History to record statements made by participants in the fight for freedom.

In the course of his interviews O'Malley collected a vast amount of local lore around Ireland. In 1952 he wrote a series of articles for *The Kerryman*, but then withdrew them before publication. Instead he used the articles for a series of talks on Radio Éireann in 1953. Subsequently those lectures were published in a series called *IRA Raids* in *The Sunday Press* in 1955–56. In the meantime he used the interviews to add to his own Civil War memoir, *The Singing Flame*, published posthumously in 1978, and to write a biographical memoir of a local Longford Republican organiser, Seán Connolly, entitled *Rising Out: Seán Connolly of Longford, 1890–1921*, also published posthumously, in 2007.

O'Malley was familiar with interviewing people about folklore and was well read in Irish and international folklore traditions. In the early 1940s he took down over 300 folktales from around his home area in Clew Bay, County Mayo. He also collected ballads and stories about the 1916–23 period. His method for his military interviews was to write rapidly in a first series of notebooks as his informant was speaking and then to rewrite his notes more coherently into a second series of notebooks. Occasionally he would include diagrams of the site of an ambush or an attack on a barracks. Given his overall knowledge of the period, based on his own Tan War activities and his Civil War responsibilities, he usually commanded a high regard from his informants. He felt that his former comrades would talk to him and tell him the truth.

From an examination of his interviews, O'Malley does not appear to have used a consistent technique, but rather he allowed his informant to ramble and cover many topics. In his rewrite of an interview he often labelled paragraphs such as Tan War, Truce, Civil War, Gaols, Treatment of Prisoners, RIC, IRB, Spies, Round-ups and the like. The tone is conversational, allowing the narrative to unfold. He wrote down the names of people and places phonetically rather than correctly. The interviews are fresh and frank and many of these men's stories may never have been told even to their children, as they did not speak openly about those times. Family members have said they could hear the voices of their relatives speaking through the O'Malley interviews, because O'Malley had been able to capture their intonations and phrasing so clearly about matters never discussed in the family before.

This present volume includes eight O'Malley interviews

covering the activities of the Cork No. 3 Brigade in West Cork and Donegal during the War of Independence, the Truce and the Civil War. All of these Cork men rejected the Treaty and so their interviews reflect strong Republican opinions. Four of these men also made statements to the Bureau of Military History.

In transcribing O'Malley's series of interviews some modest changes have been made to help the reader better understand the interview. To enable reference to O'Malley's original pagination, his pages are referred to in bold brackets, such as [17L], the L or R representing the left or right side of his original page. O'Malley often wrote on the right-hand page of a notebook first and then moved on to the left. Extensive footnotes provide a better understanding of the people, places and incidents involved, and some are repeated in more than one chapter to allow each chapter to be read separately as a complete story. The original text has been largely revised to include correct spellings of names and places, although some errors in general grammar and punctuation have been reproduced. O'Malley regularly inserted his own comments in parentheses, and these are reflected in this volume in italics following the abbreviation EOM for the sake of clarity. Some editorial comments or clarifications have been added in square brackets.

Each interview has been reproduced here in full. In some places O'Malley left blank spaces where he was missing information, and these are represented by ellipses. Ellipses have also been used to indicate where the original text is indecipherable. The style of local phrasing used in the interviews has been retained, some of which is no longer in common usage and may read strangely to the modern reader. In some instances O'Malley included names and facts that do not seem fully relevant but these have been retained in order to maintain the integrity of the original interview.

We have relied on the integrity of O'Malley's general knowledge of facts and his ability to question and ascertain the 'truth', but clearly it is possible that the details related here to O'Malley reflect only the perceptions of the individual informant rather than the absolute historical truth, and the reader must appreciate this important subtlety. Also these interviews do not give a complete account of the role played by each individual during this period.

In the case of West Cork, O'Malley interviewed his informants only once and so there is little duplication within each interview, but several of the men do speak about the same incidents and naturally there are some differences between their versions. This illustrates clearly how one incident can be viewed differently by different people. Although O'Malley was not actually involved in any of the West Cork or Donegal activities recorded in these interviews, he must have heard stories about them over the years, but clearly there are some subjects that he did not venture to record.

For those not familiar with the structure of military organisations such as the IRA during this period, it might be helpful to know that the largest unit was a division, which consisted of several brigades, each of which had several battalions, which in turn were composed of several companies at the local level. There were usually staff functions, such as intelligence and quartermaster roles, at division, brigade and battalion levels, and usually only officers at the company level.

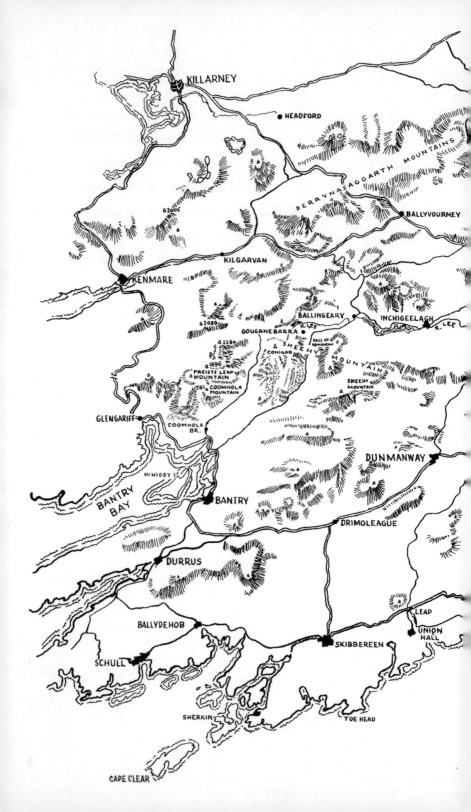

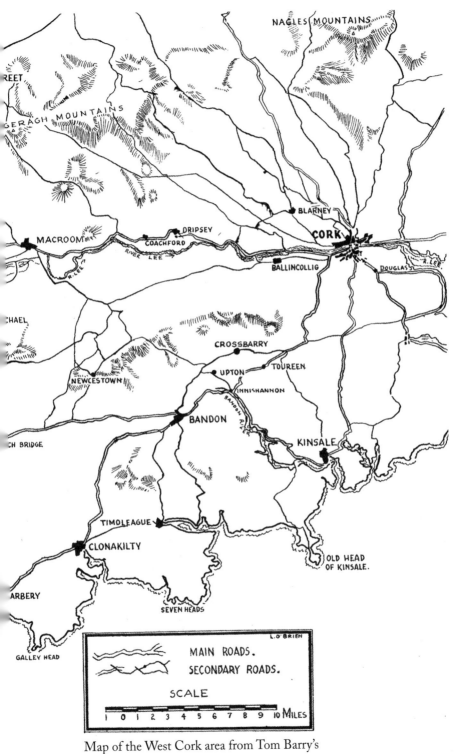

Map of the West Cork area from Tom Barry's *Guerilla Days in Ireland*.

Map of County Donegal. (*Courtesy of Mercier Press*)

INTRODUCTION

Historical memory of the Irish revolutionary period has for many years awarded a special place to the Irish Republican Army's West Cork (Cork No. 3) Brigade. While the justice of this position can be debated, West Cork's prominence remains well established within the popular imagination. The area is notable for many critical events and compelling personalities. It is probably best known for hosting two highly significant sites of nationalist commemoration that reflect both sides of the Civil War divide: Kilmichael and Béal na mBláth. Both of these sites hosted episodes that have generated long-running and heated debates and competing theories over what actually happened, as well as highly politicised commemorative events.

The celebration of West Cork can be traced to the emergence of a first wave of mainly Republican histories of the conflict period. The publication of *Rebel Cork's Fighting Story 1916–1921* in 1947 drew attention to major and also relatively forgotten episodes in West Cork, as part of the wider coverage of the entire county. However, the release of Tom Barry's *Guerilla Days in Ireland* in 1949 dramatically increased public awareness of West Cork. Indeed, that memoir quickly became the most iconic and widely read account of the Irish War of Independence. With its heavy emphasis on Tom Barry's leadership and the activities of his flying column, it detailed the Republican's most successful military episodes from an IRA perspective. Barry's egocentric perspective was further indulged in Ewan Butler's *Barry's Flying Column: The Story of the IRA's Cork No. 3 Brigade*, in 1972.

However, that narrative focus was challenged to some degree the following year by Liam Deasy's memoir, *Towards Ireland Free: the West Cork Brigade in the War of Independence 1917–1921*. Deasy's more extensively researched account widened the focus to the entire brigade area and covered the neglected years between 1916 and 1919. The book quickly received a scathing denunciation from Tom Barry in his pamphlet, *The Reality of the Anglo-Irish War 1920–1921 in West Cork: Refutations, Corrections, and Comments on Liam Deasy's Towards Ireland Free*. Barry objected to a number of Deasy's interpretations of events, which differed from his own, most notably the 'false surrender' at the Kilmichael Ambush. Published shortly after Deasy's death, this pamphlet brought to the surface many of the tensions that had existed between the brigade leadership since the War of Independence. Some of that personal animosity is also readily apparent in the accounts published in this book, which are based on the interviews and notes of Ernie O'Malley undertaken between 1949 and 1956. This book shows that long before the 1970s, elements of the history of the Irish revolution in West Cork were contested by some of the key Republican protagonists.

This bias towards focusing on West Cork can be seen in more recent publications too. Although Peter Hart's *The IRA and Its Enemies: Violence and Community in Cork 1916–1923* (published in 1998) was a county-based study, the key case study chapters focused heavily on West Cork. This attention on West Cork can be seen again in David Fitzpatrick's edited collection, *Terror in Ireland 1916–1923* (dedicated to the memory of Peter Hart). Although it encompassed studies of violence across the island, it is noteworthy that the two Cork chapters again focused entirely on West Cork (one on Kilmichael and one on spies and informers), taking up themes which both Tom Barry and Peter Hart had engaged with in much detail.

However, with the public release of the Bureau of Military History (BMH) witness statements (WS), our knowledge of the Irish revolution throughout the county, and indeed the country, has advanced. These statements provide another layer of evidence from the perspective of both the volunteers and the military elite. The West Cork testimony features statements from senior figures like Florry Begley, Liam Deasy, Maurice 'Mossy' Donegan and Ted O'Sullivan, who also appear in this book. These individuals willingly participated in the bureau's project to construct a public history of the revolution. However, this book also includes material from IRA veterans who did not cooperate with the Bureau – Stephen O'Neill, Billy O'Sullivan, Barney O'Driscoll and Jack Fitzgerald. Thus, the Ernie O'Malley notebooks offer valuable veteran testimony not available elsewhere. In addition, while the BMH witness statements generally stop at the Truce of 1921, O'Malley's interviews also cover the Civil War years.

The O'Malley interviews are found in a series of notebooks kept in the University College Dublin Archives (UCDA). Up until 2012 public access to this testimony had been limited to researchers who were willing to attempt to decipher his notoriously difficult handwriting. However, a recent project to transcribe and publish the interviews, undertaken by Mercier Press and Cormac O'Malley, is gradually bringing the contents of the notebooks to a far wider audience. This series of books constitutes part of an array of new sources now available on the revolutionary period.

Owing to the great number of interviews conducted by Ernie O'Malley in County Cork, we have broken with the county focus adopted so far in the series and divided County Cork into sub-regions. This first volume for the county focuses on the area constituting the West Cork (Cork No. 3) Brigade, from the point when it was established in 1919. Additional volumes will contain interviews from the men of North Cork (Cork No. 2 and No. 4 Brigades), Mid-Cork and Cork city (Cork No. 1 Brigade). We have included all the West Cork interviews bar one (a very brief conversation with Ralph Keyes, a former battalion commander in the Bantry area).

During the War of Independence, the Cork No. 3 Brigade comprised seven battalions: 1st (Bandon); 2nd (Clonakilty);

3rd (Dunmanway); 4th (Skibbereen); 5th (Bantry); 6th (Castletownbere) and 7th (Schull). During the Truce period, the brigade was subdivided and reorganised, with the new Cork No. 5 Brigade established along the far western part of the county. Cork No. 5 Brigade was made up of five battalions: 1st (Schull); 2nd (Skibbereen); 3rd (Drimoleague); 4th (Bantry); and 5th (Castletownbere).

Ernie O'Malley's interviews with former IRA activists were held roughly a quarter of a century after the end of the Civil War. These conversations were conducted and transcribed by O'Malley, thus forming a rough draft of a Republican oral history of the military campaign, especially during the Civil War. The voices of the interview subjects are clearly heard. The narrative is episodic and personalised, with the interviewee at the centre of most of the events recounted. However, O'Malley's influence over the interviews can also be seen – he decided who to interview, who to exclude, what subjects the conversations focused on and what subjects were omitted. The voices heard in these notebooks are thus filtered through O'Malley. That should not diminish their value, but it does require readers to approach this material critically.

We also wish to add an important disclaimer to our transcription. It reflects the best efforts of three period specialists to decipher O'Malley's appalling writing. Anyone familiar with the O'Malley notebooks can sympathise with the difficult task of creating a reliable transcription. In some places we have added words in square brackets to make grammatical sense of the transcription and in some places have added a suggestion with a question mark where we are uncertain about what has been transcribed by O'Malley. Readers should be aware, though, that mistakes are easy to make, and occasionally the effort depends on informed guesswork. We advise any readers relying on a specific passage of this book for an important argument to return to the source material at the UCD Archives and confirm the exact transcription themselves.

Overall, Ernie O'Malley interviewed approximately 450 people in the course of his project, out of a mass movement of up to 100,000 members across the island. His interview subjects were a tiny and fairly unrepresentative sample. From the O'Malley interviews published so far, we can see that a very high percentage of them were very senior IRA officers at the top of the organisation. Roughly 25 per cent of the conversations occurred with commanders of either an IRA brigade or a division, placing them in charge of hundreds or thousands of Volunteers. As the IRA was a decentralised organisation, O'Malley probably wanted to capture the geographic variance in different locales. He sought testimony from those in the best position to understand the conflict: the top military commanders and their staff officers. Voices from the strictly political or civilian end are almost entirely missing from his conversations. Members of Sinn Féin and the underground Dáil Éireann administration are absent, except when they were also leading figures in the IRA. We hear nothing from those involved in Republican humanitarian groups such as the White Cross. Ordinary supporters of the Republicans, who donated funds, opened their homes to fugitives and boycotted the British state, do not have a place here. Similarly, Irish trade unionists are excluded.

The military narrative itself is shaped by those interviewed by O'Malley. We hear largely from top military commanders who were opposed to the Anglo-Irish Treaty and were active fighters during the Civil War. Largely absent are those who dropped out, who refused to fight, who withdrew from the IRA or who joined the Free State Army or the neutral IRA. Perhaps most remarkable is the lack of women interviewed. This series is appropriately called *The Men Will Talk to Me*, as Cumann na mBan is almost entirely missing from these conversations. The handful of women interviewed usually acted as witnesses of atrocities committed on Republican men. Overall, O'Malley seems to have the greatest interest in IRA hardliners: Éamon de Valera's 'legion of the rearguard'.

The O'Malley interview transcripts only sometimes include O'Malley's questions. However, we should assume he was asking questions throughout these conversations. The reappearance of certain common themes reflects O'Malley's direction. He appeared drawn to material that informed his own research interests. The project seems in some ways a personal journey for O'Malley to better understand the Republican defeat in

1922–23. His questions and the subject matter covered reflect his own views as a participant in the Irish revolution, as well as his role as its historian and witness. Leadership is frequently explored, with contributors offering candid assessments of different officers. O'Malley's interest in this subject may have stemmed from his service as an IRA headquarters organiser, where he frequently assessed individuals' capacity for command. By seeking such judgement from the contributors, he seemed to want to link individuals with local military performances. There are also frequent questions about the functions of the Irish Republican Brotherhood (IRB), especially in regards to its impact on the Anglo-Irish Treaty split. O'Malley was not a member of the IRB, so he had little personal understanding of its internal workings and seemed to want to educate himself as to the importance of the IRB in the division of the IRA over the Treaty. He may have been influenced in this by Republican propaganda depicting the Treaty split as essentially an IRB plot to seize control of the government.

Assessments of the IRA general headquarters staff generally, and Michael Collins specifically, also often appear in these interviews. O'Malley seems to be fascinated by Collins' emergence as the Civil War strongman. Particular attention is paid to attempts by Collins and his inner circle to recruit officers into the new National Army. O'Malley appears to be interested in whether this was done unethically. He also tries to draw out information about the shooting of suspected civilian informers. This interest predates the intense scrutiny this aspect of the revolution has received from modern historians. O'Malley's own memoir, *On Another Man's Wound*, reveals how deeply he was affected by his shooting of three captured British soldiers.

Interviewees were frequently queried about the attitude of the Catholic Church in their areas. This seems particularly relevant to the deteriorating political position of Republicans and their general loss of communal legitimacy during the Civil War. O'Malley also often explored the different peace moves that occurred after he was imprisoned. He was especially interested in Liam Deasy's unilateral call for a ceasefire in January 1923 and the assumption that this may have led to a general Republican collapse.

Prison narratives are emphasised throughout these testimonies. O'Malley concentrates on the torture endured by certain activists, even securing supporting statements from other witnesses in some instances. Again, this focus is not surprising, considering that O'Malley himself was captured twice, tortured, escaped from jail and undertook a hunger strike. He gives prominence to the systemic aspect of the Republican prison experience so often ignored by historians.

There are just eight interview subjects in this book, which seems scant considering the importance attributed in the literature to West Cork's role in the Irish revolution. Tom Barry probably had a major influence here, specifically the 1949 release of *Guerilla Days in Ireland*, which occurred just as O'Malley was beginning his interviews. O'Malley seems to have avoided ground already covered by Barry's narrative, which focuses on the area around Bandon. Five of these eight interview subjects operated outside the Bandon Battalion, which had been the most dominant battalion in the West Cork Brigade. The dynamic IRA leader Seán Lehane also takes a central role in much of the narrative, rescuing a critical figure from neglect. The interviews give prominence to the far western coastal portions of the Cork No. 3 Brigade area (largely organised by Lehane), which was reconstituted as the Cork No. 5 Brigade during the Truce period.

Five of the eight subjects participated in the IRA's campaign in Ulster. They basically comprised the Cork leadership element of the northern campaign in early 1922, with three of the interviewees serving as brigade commanders there. Their testimony describes the campaign from its inception, which seemed to be of particular interest to O'Malley. In his interviews outside Cork, he frequently asked individuals elsewhere if their anti-Treaty unit participated in a rifle exchange with the National Army. This occurred secretly in May 1922, as Free State rifles supplied by Britain were swapped with IRA rifles, which were then sent to arm the IRA in Ulster. This level of close cooperation was little known outside the IRA at the time of the O'Malley interviews, though it became public knowledge after the release of Florrie O'Donoghue's biography of Liam Lynch, *No Other Law*, in 1956.

The West Cork interviews seem to have been conducted specifically to detail the IRA's intervention in Ulster, as well as to give prominence to the Cork No. 5 Brigade. O'Malley may have also wanted to document the gruesome torture of Cork No. 5 Brigade commander Ted O'Sullivan, which he had become aware of when in prison.

The last of the interviews in the book is with Liam Deasy, whose Civil War surrender both appalled and fascinated O'Malley. The lack of a proper transcription of that conversation, which is unique in this book, may reflect O'Malley's own difficulties carrying out a conversation on such a critical and contested subject. This was the least successful dialogue in this book, characterised by poor note-taking, a less continuous narrative, and the lack of a second draft transcription (which was evident in the other interviews). The contrast is greatest with the Florry Begley interview. Though constrained by Begley's unwillingness to allow notes to be taken during the interview (O'Malley later made his first transcription of Begley's comments from memory), the writing and order of the narrative in this instance was much clearer than in the other interviews. A more successful rapport between interviewer and subject is reflected in the quality, depth and length of the Ted O'Sullivan interview. Overall, the written outcomes of all the conversations were influenced by the quality of the relationship that developed between O'Malley and his subject during the course of the interview.

Considering the historiography of Cork and the revolution, O'Malley's West Cork interviews are striking for what they omit. The interviews seldom mention the Kilmichael Ambush; there is no discussion of the so-called Bandon Valley massacre; and there is little talk of Béal na mBláth and the killing of Michael Collins. One could speculate that such topics might have been considered too sensitive to discuss. However, when considering the O'Malley interviews as a whole, a more likely explanation is that O'Malley did not think those events were critical to the overall Republican narrative.

There is also little discussion of the inner workings of the three IRA conventions of 1922, which split the army into three factions. We hear almost nothing about the IRA's ruling executive and O'Malley seems uninterested in IRA headquarters policy, which he himself helped shape. He had probably already settled in his own mind his explanation for these events, and thus felt little need to collect additional material about them.

O'Malley was trying to accomplish a number of things with these interviews. One was to add missing voices to the Irish revolutionary narrative, especially from the anti-Treaty IRA military elite. Secondly, he was trying to gather further information for his own work as a historian, filling in the blanks in order to construct new explanations of the IRA's defeat (something of a Republican post-mortem). These interviews, undertaken and transcribed in the final decade of O'Malley's life, probably signal his intention to add another layer to what became *The Singing Flame*, or to write a Civil War version of *Raids and Rallies*. Finally, and perhaps most importantly, at the core of this endeavour lay O'Malley's burning desire to understand what he had experienced during two wars. He felt compelled to ascertain what he had missed while on active service or during imprisonment, and to gain a deeper and wider appreciation of the spectacular events he had lived through, witnessed and ultimately survived.

James Bernard 'Barney' O'Driscoll

(UCDA P17b/95, pp. 16–21)

Barney O'Driscoll (1891–1961) was born in Castletownsend, raised in Skibbereen, and educated at St Coleman's College in Fermoy. In 1908 he emigrated to the United States, and during his five-year stay he immersed himself in Republican activities. Upon his return to West Cork, he entered the quarry business, and also helped establish Sinn Féin and the Irish

Courtesy of Barbara O'Driscoll

Volunteers in his district. He endured several prison terms for Republican activities, and was finally released from jail in 1922. He stayed largely neutral in the Civil War, opening Killaloe Slate Quarry Company in 1923. From the slate quarrying business, he moved into plastic and metal manufacturing, becoming one of the country's leading industrialists. He developed a number of metal and plastic factories in Clare and Tipperary, partnering with major international firms. O'Driscoll settled with his wife and children in Nenagh, County Tipperary. Dying in 1961, his large funeral attendance included President Éamon de Valera.

***

[16R] 1910. Paddy Ford[1] of the *Irish World* was a very strong supporter of the AOH.[2] They were trying to capture the 69th Regiment for the AOH.[3] The Clan na Gael,[4] the non-military side, controlled the Irish Volunteers [USA] who were trying to control the 69th 1st Regiment of the Irish Volunteer Society in New York and the second [regiment] in Brooklyn, the 14th National Guard then in Brooklyn.[5] We tried to control it for I was a member of the Irish Volunteers, and we had H Company, [with] a good few Irish in it, the captain, a German friendly to the Irish. The carrying of arms was then permitted in the USA provided you carried them openly. We went for route marches. We bought our own rifles and ammunition. We went out to ranges in the country for rifle practice. Up to 1914 the AOH

1   Irish-American Patrick Ford published the nationalist *Irish World* newspaper in New York.

2   The Ancient Order of Hibernians (AOH) is a Catholic political association founded in America in 1836. The group's aims are to support Irish independence and promote the Catholic faith. It has often been described as a 'Green' version of the Orange Order. In the early 1900s the AOH in Ireland was allied to John Redmond's Irish Parliamentary Party and used violence to silence political opponents and criticism of the party. There were frequent violent clashes between Irish Republicans and Hibernians during the Irish War of Independence, particularly in Ulster.

3   The 69th Regiment was a National Guard (military reserve) unit in New York city. The 'Fighting 69th' was closely associated with the city's Irish-American population and became a celebrated American formation during the First World War.

4   Clan na Gael was a Republican organisation in the United States established by the Fenians. It acted as a sister organisation to the IRB in Ireland.

5   The 14th Regiment was also a National Guard (military reserve) unit in New York. O'Driscoll is describing his experiences in the United States before the outbreak of the First World War.

controlled the 69th. You had to be a member of the Clan before you could become a member of the Irish Volunteers. Our leader was Martin L. Biggale.

I was in Frongoch in 1916 as Q[uarter] Master.[6] We checked out the rations every day at the railway station about 300 yards away, three times a day. I got a letter from home which had been sent there from a cousin of mine – Armour & Co. of Chicago – who was manager in Liverpool. His name was Cruickshank. He had a lot of corned beef, and he, being an imperialist and not knowing my sympathies, had written me a letter offering to give me some barrels cheap. My mother had sent on the letter. I asked Mick Staines, our Camp Commandant, if I could send out **[17L]** a business letter.[7] He gave me permission but the Camp authorities refused it. I wrote a letter [and] gave it to one of the RDC's, Royal Defence Corps, men of above military age who helped to guard us. He posted it. Next we had a wholesale line out for letters. In public, to take away suspicion, I was particularly nasty to this man. I used to abuse him, for the British were then looking out for our sources. There was a large store where we received provisions. I had the letters in my pocket addressed to an English address with Irish letters inside. He came up behind

6   Frongoch was an internment camp in north Wales situated in a disused whiskey distillery. The British government initially opened the camp to hold German soldiers taken prisoner in the First World War, but after the 1916 Rising it was used to intern nearly 2,000 Irish Republicans. The camp was closed in December 1916 and the internees were released.

7   Michael Staines was a senior member of the Irish Volunteers and a TD in the First Dáil.

me, took out the letters, dropped them into a half-full tea chest. Always there was a little money for himself. The British put a detective, who, in the local post office, opened our letters for Ireland, but he never found our letters.

Brennan-Whitmore knew of one method of getting information out, through cigarette cartoons.[8] He drew a sketch of this in his book on Frongoch and I must say if [he] had known anything about our way of sending, he would also have mentioned it.

IRB in Frongoch: Michael Collins started it. Gearóid O'Sullivan was weak and thin at the time.[9] We put him between us in bed to keep him warm. Then in the Camp was Colm O'Murchada.[10] He also was a member.

[17R] Seán Ó Muirthile wasn't there.[11] He started life as an auxiliary postman in Leap, County Cork. Some letters were missing and he was responsible. He was dismissed. His father and mother were native Irish speakers. He became a native Irish organiser. For years Michael Collins loathed him. Gearóid

---

8   W. J. Brennan-Whitmore was an officer of the Irish Volunteers during the Easter Rising and author of *With the Irish in Frongoch* (Cork 2013).

9   Gearóid O'Sullivan was adjutant-general of the IRA during the War of Independence, a position he also served in the National Army during the Civil War.

10   Colm O'Murchada (not O'Murathu as in the original text), a loyal supporter of Michael Collins, was acting secretary to the cabinet in 1921. At the crucial late night meeting of 3 December 1921, he made cryptic and inadequate notes about the details of the impending Anglo-Irish Treaty.

11   Seán Ó Muirthile was a top figure in the IRB. In the Civil War he served as quartermaster general in the National Army with the rank of lieutenant general.

[O'Sullivan] had no mind of his own. He copied Mick Collins.

Diarmuid O'Hegarty was arrested in 1916.[12] A question was asked about a John Hegarty in the House of Commons. He had been wrongfully arrested. The prison warder came to Diarmuid in prison. 'Are you John Hegarty?' he asked.

'No, I'm not,' replied Diarmuid O'Hegarty.

'Well, what does Diarmuid mean in English?'

'It's not John, anyhow.'

The warder went away. He returned. 'Are you sure your name is not John?'

'Yes, I'm sure.'

He came back. 'Well John or no John, pack up and get to hell out of this.'

When Diarmuid came back to the Department of Agriculture, T. P. Gill sent for him.[13] He had known that Diarmuid had been out in the Rising. 'Take your holidays first, Hegarty,' he said, 'and report back. I hope you enjoyed the time you were fighting.'

Frongoch: [One] November day we decided to burn our camp. We had sent out so many complaints about the Brewery where we had been stationed that in the end the British were

---

12   Diarmuid O'Hegarty was a senior leader of both the military and political wings of the independence movement, and was closely associated with Michael Collins and the pro-Treaty military elite.

13   Thomas Patrick Gill was a journalist and Home Rule and Land War politician. He was the first manager of the Department of Agriculture and Technical Instruction from 1900 to 1923.

ordered to put us in one camp.[14] That was our loss for the camp was bitterly cold, full of mud and dirt. We were kept out **[18L]** in the open that snowy day. The British put out the fires we had lighted in the huts. The sergeant major, 'Jackknives', picked out 7 of us including myself for punishment. We were made [to] stand outside, a soldier in charge of each of us, who never let us get out of his sight. Two more soldiers were added and an NCO. We were taken off by train. No food for us or the soldiers all that day: eventually we reached Reading Gaol.

I was given a fine bed, a beautiful clean cell and good food. We were kept in the women's prison. There were 35 of our men all told there. Reading Gaol had been used by the British for spies or for Irish, foreigners, whoever they weren't sure of: Chinese, Dutch, etc. amongst them. The food cooked in the male prison was brought over by some of these foreigners. Amongst them was a Dutchman who was always complaining about being in gaol as his country was neutral. He talked to Arthur Griffith about his trouble.[15] He was accustomed to go to and fro on Dutch boats. 'But had you no passport?' said Griffith.

'Oh indeed I had a passport,' he said, 'why I had seven of them.'

Amongst the men there were Seán T. O'Kelly, Tommy MacCurtain, Ernest Blythe, Walter Cole, Terry MacSwiney,

14   Part of Frongoch Camp was built over a disused distillery (not a brewery), where the prisoners initially slept.

15   Arthur Griffith was a journalist and a founding member of Sinn Féin. He would later be the senior figure in the pro-Treaty political movement.

Henry Dixon, [18R] ?Harry Cotton, George Nichols of Galway, Darrell Figgis, Éamon Dwyer of Goulds Cross [Tipperary].[16] There was no mention of IRB then in this prison.

1921: Henry Dixon and I, both of us had been in the US.[17] We both thought the trouble between Devoy and Cohalan had been most probably due to Dev.[18] The AOH had been very strong. There were at least 9 AOH men for every Clan man. Ford had been AOH, of course, but in 1916 he changed over, becoming more extreme even than Devoy.[19] John Devoy, deep in his own bitterness, didn't want Dev to link up with Ford or his group. Dev said he couldn't afford not to use, to neglect, any Irishman who could be of use to the country.

---

16   Seán T. O'Kelly was a founding member of Sinn Féin and later president of Ireland; Tomás MacCurtain was a co-founder of the Irish Volunteers in Cork and later Lord Mayor of Cork; Ernest Blythe was an Ulster-born separatist involved in the IRB and the Irish Volunteers; Liverpool-born Walter Cole was one of Sinn Féin's first elected officials (alderman on Dublin Corporation); Terence MacSwiney was a key leader in Cork who later died on hunger strike; George Nichols was a veteran IRB leader in Galway; Darrell Figgis was a writer and Sinn Féin activist; Éamon Dwyer was a leader of the Irish Volunteers in Tipperary. No information was available for Harry Cotton.

17   Henry Dixon was a veteran separatist who co-founded Sinn Féin in 1905.

18   John Devoy and Judge Daniel Cohalan were leaders of the Irish-American Republican organisation, Clan na Gael. Devoy and Cohalan ran the Friends of Irish Freedom organisation, and clashed with Éamon de Valera during his efforts to secure US government recognition of the Irish Republic. In 1920, frustrated with his lack of control over the Friends of Irish Freedom, de Valera established a rival organisation, the American Association for the Recognition of the Irish Republic, which was closely associated with Dáil Éireann.

19   Patrick Ford, publisher of the *Irish World* in New York.

Daniel Cohalan was a believer first of all in Cohalan, and then his interest was Irish-American politics. (EOM: *Liam Mellows, according to Andy Doyle, had had a row with Devoy when he went to the US in 1917*).[20] Devoy was very bitter. He had been more bitter to O'Donovan Rossa than he had been to Dev. Rossa was a dynamiter. He didn't believe in going into the field, but he wanted to blow up buildings in England to carry the war into their country. My cousin was married to Rossa. His mind was going when he died. Rossa was able to keep his mind alive in gaol by never accepting anything **[19L]** from his enemies. He made them fight back not that they wanted any excuse, but they were made to suit his quarrels. He always rubbed the warders the wrong way.

Frongoch: 'Jackknives', the sergeant major, had a terrible tongue, but he had a heart of gold. At one time there were a couple of calls each day, roll calls, and then they called out the men's numbers, not their name. One day the officer was calling the numbers: WO 1246, 'anseo'.[21] WO 1924, 'anseo'. WO 2132, 'anseo', WO 146, no reply. 146, no reply. Jackknives began to roar, 'No. 146!' Again, 'No. 146!' Slowly, through the crowd pushed his way Jack Hughes, a huge man who could throw any 4 military police around him. Jackknives was a big powerful man.

---

20 Following the Easter Rising, Liam Mellows took refuge in the United States. Andy Doyle, incorrectly spelled Andie in the original, was an officer in the Dublin Brigade.

21 Anseo, not annseo as in the original text, is the Irish for here.

'What do you want?' asked Jack Hughes.

Jackknives bent forward and said in a polite whisper, '… why didn't you answer your name?'

There was a Lieutenant Douglas there. Perhaps he was a Lord Alfred Douglas and a relation of Oscar Wilde.[22] He was always kind and sympathetic to us. The adjutant was Lieutenant Byrnes, a regular of between 40–45 years of age. A very intelligent man, indeed. Henry Dixon said 7 or 8 years ago, there was a Lipton Canteen Scandal and **[19R]** there was a Major Byrnes there.[23] I bet he is the man. We had some meat one morning. The meat was rancid. Collins and Staines advised me to put it in a warm place so that it would be thoroughly rotten in a few hours time when the major would inspect it. And so it was. Byrnes said to me, 'You can wash it in vinegar. It'll do.'

'I won't,' I said, 'this is not Lipton now.'

He raised his stick as if to hit me, but he controlled himself and ever afterwards he was polite and agreeable to me.

When we reached Frongoch the place had been previously occupied by German prisoners of war, some of whom must have been tubercular. The British had cleared out the camps but they left untouched a large stack of envelopes marked Prisoner of War on the outside. We used these for a time before it was discovered.

22 The officer was not Lord Alfred Douglas, who was at the centre of Oscar Wilde's libel action against Douglas' father, the Marquess of Queensberry.

23 This was a corruption case concerning food contractor Lipton paying bribes to numerous British Army officers managing military canteens. One of the defendants was Lieutenant James Burns of the 8th Hussars.

Questions were asked about it in the House of Commons, and as a result we claimed prisoner of war rights and treatment.

When released I went to West Cork. There was a vessel wrecked on the island off my coast. I found a revolver in the captain's cabin. I showed it to Mick Collins who was then on a visit to West Cork. He took the revolver.

(EOM: *Collins, was he a bully?*)

I don't know, but if you were ever in trouble he was a good man to have near you.

[20] I was 2 months in jail with Arthur Griffith. He thought that there would be no further need for fighting, that the blood spilt in 1916 had played its part and that there was now no need for more. I thought he was callous about the execution of Casement.[24] He was hoping that they would execute Casement, for if they didn't hang him then Irish people would say that he had been a [British] spy.

Mick Collins: A fast man to read and he read a lot. He not only knew poetry, but he could quote it. We had a fierce argument once about 'Kelly and Burke and Shea', as to who wrote it, and I think I was right.[25] He knew some of R. W. Service by heart.[26]

---

24   Roger Casement, a leading Irish separatist, was arrested in County Kerry after being landed at Banna Strand from a German submarine on 21 April 1916. He had been in Germany trying to form an Irish Brigade from Irish prisoners of war taken by the Germans during the First World War. He was hung for high treason at Pentonville Prison, London, on 3 August 1916.

25   'Kelly, Burke and Shea', a poem celebrating Irish nationalists' martial qualities, was written by Joseph Ignatius Constantine Clarke in 1898.

26   Robert William Service was a popular British-Canadian poet, best

Cork was controlled by Mick Collins. Bishop Cohalan in Cork was very pro-Treaty.[27] He went very hard on Dónal Óg to vote for the Treaty and it was said that he made him a promise to vote for it.[28] 'I don't believe that,' said Andy Doyle, for Dónal Óg wouldn't give his word lightly. Bishop Kelly [was] very anti-Sinn Féin in West Cork.[29] He kept a good grip on his priests. One of them, Fr Eugene Daly, a friend of mine, in favour of the IRA and of Sinn Féin. In 1919 there was some Blessed Oliver Plunkett celebration.[30] He referred to the venerable Oliver, then mentioned his descendants, talking of Plunkett, Count Plunkett. This Fr Daly was put on an [21] interdict, not to refer to anything in the nature of politics.

There is a big percentage of Protestants in West Cork and a very close association with the British Navy. These two big influences were at work. Get a woman who would have 2 sons in the British Navy who would be completely loyal to the Republic, or to the boys.

known for his poems set in the Canadian Yukon gold rush at the turn of the century, such as 'The Shooting of Dan McGrew' and 'The Cremation of Sam McGee'.

27   Bishop Daniel Cohalan, Catholic bishop of the Cork diocese, excommunicated IRA fighters in December 1920 and was strongly anti-Republican during the Civil War.

28   Donal Óg O'Callaghan was a Republican activist who succeeded Terence MacSwiney as lord mayor of Cork.

29   Denis Kelly, Catholic bishop of Ross (West Cork), was a strong Redmondite and persistent critic of the Republicans.

30   Irish Archbishop Oliver Plunkett was declared a martyr of the faith by the Catholic Church in 1918, beatified in 1920 and canonised as a saint in 1975.

Influence of priests was then very strong. Much stronger than it is now.

Cork in 1909 had O'Brienites who to a man went over to Sinn Féin, and this was a seed, [an] anti-Redmondite seed, and this helped West Cork.[31]

West Cork: Ancient Order of Hibernians, Redmondite crowd. AOH American Alliance, which was backed by the O'Brien crowd.

Private meeting in Cork held by Mick Collins of his supporters at which Collins advocated the breaking of the Pact.[32] O'Driscoll was against this action of Michael [Collins].[33] Church holiday in Cork on that occasion and a parade. Cathal Brugha not consulted as he was Minister of Defence.

(EOM: *Was Griffith jealous of Dev?*)

Darrell Figgis and the Constitution.[34] Darrell a friend of Griffith.

---

31   Followers of William O'Brien's All For Ireland League, a party which appealed to rural and urban labourers and militant nationalists. It also preached conciliation towards unionists.
32   The Collins/de Valera Pact for the June 1922 general election. The night before the election, while speaking in Cork city, Michael Collins told supporters to vote for whomever they wished rather than the Sinn Féin election panel, thereby breaking his agreement with de Valera.
33   Barney O'Driscoll – O'Malley seems to be summarising what O'Driscoll has said here.
34   Darrell Figgis, a Sinn Féin pioneer and co-founder of the Irish Volunteers, supported the Anglo-Irish Treaty and served as vice-chairman of the committee that wrote the Free State constitution. He opposed the Collins/de Valera Pact during the June 1922 general election, in which he successfully ran as a pro-Treaty independent.

STEPHEN O'NEILL

(UCDA P17b/112, pp. 103–108)

Stephen O'Neill (1891–1966) was born and raised in Clonakilty. A key member of the Cork No. 3 Brigade flying column, he participated in numerous actions before his capture in 1921. During the Civil War he fought with the Republican forces and was jailed for a second time. Following his release, O'Neill became a building contractor. He ultimately relocated to Castleisland, County Kerry. O'Neill wrote an account of the Kilmichael Ambush for the 1937 edition of *Rebel Cork's Fighting Story*. In later years he frequently attended Republican commemorations of the revolutionary period. He passed away just three days before the major 1966 commemoration of the Kilmichael Ambush. His wife attended in his place. He is buried in Kilmurray, County Cork.

***

[103R] I belonged to Clonakilty Company. We were on the run for we had attacked Clonakilty CGS [Coast Guard Station] where we had captured 2 rifles but we were picked up. Seán [Lehane] was from Bantry and he had been with the West Cork column for 2 or 3 weeks before Christmas [1920] and he

took charge of it when Tom Barry got sick.[1] We were brought
first to Bandon, but there they didn't seem to understand about
us. The RIC were surprised when they got us, but they didn't
know I had been with the Column. Flyer [Nyhan] and I were
never touched when we were in Bandon.[2] There was an Auxie
who survived the Kilmichael Ambush and fellows in Cork
Gaol had been taken up for him so that he could identify them,
but although we had both been at Kilmichael, we were not
brought before him.[3] This Auxie had gone off his head. From
Cork we were brought to Ballykinlar by sea.[4] We had a very
decent escort. It was a Sunday, a grand day. 'Will you leave
us on deck?' we asked, so they left us on deck all day. They
gave us plenty of bacon and cigarettes for some of them were
Irish and a Wexford fellow, a sailor, gave me £5 to give to Dáil
Éireann funds and he took any letters we had written and he
promised to post them for us. When we reached the dockyards
in Belfast some of the workers came out and they attacked us.

1   Seán Lehane, a senior figure in the Cork No. 3 Brigade, commanded the
     Schull area and flying columns in 1920 and 1921. Tom Barry became ill
     in December 1920, with a heart problem and was laid up for most of the
     month. Lehane succeeded Liam Deasy as brigade commander during the
     Truce period, but resigned his position when Tom Hales was released
     from prison. In the Civil War, Lehane commanded Republican forces in
     Ulster during the border offensive.
2   John 'Flyer' Nyhan was a native of Clonakilty and a highly active member
     of the Cork No. 3 Brigade.
3   Cadet H. F. Forde was the sole Auxiliary survivor of the Kilmichael
     Ambush of 28 November 1920.
4   Ballykinlar Internment Camp was opened in late 1920 on the coast of
     County Down. The Royal Navy often transported Munster prisoners
     there by warship.

The military protected some of their lorries full of prisoners, but other lorries they did not protect and the men were attacked with bolts and coal. Pax Whelan was with me on that trip.[5] On the boat up **[104R]** we were not handcuffed. (EOM: *They evidently went to Belfast Gaol where they went on hunger strike and were removed by boat to England.*) I was handcuffed to Bill Lennon, from Wexford who is now dead, on my way to the [Wormwood] Scrubs and we were kept handcuffed all day.[6] As we were on hunger strike we could not take any food. (The second time I was arrested) we were saying the Rosary down below in the boat and they fired down water on top of us, for they kept us below all the time. I was sent to Ballykinlar No. 1 Camp, for the No. 2 Camp was full.

Fionán Lynch:[7] There was a tunnel in No. 1 Camp and it was just nearly finished. A certain crowd in No. 2 had been picked out for an escape and they were to go sick so that they could be removed to No. 1, for there was no hospital in No. 2 Camp. Our Camp was in the centre of a big military camp, so we stayed there until the general release in Christmas 1921. The Treaty had not been much discussed inside in the camp. We met Mick Collins in Dublin, those of us from West Cork

5 Pax Whelan, from Waterford, was a senior IRA commander in the War of Independence and Civil War.
6 Scrubs, not Scrubbs as in the original text here and elsewhere.
7 Fionán Lynch, a Kerryman associated with the Dublin IRA leadership, was a commandant-general in the National Army during the Civil War and a TD from 1918 to 1937.

who had been in the Camp – Connie Crowley, Mick [O']Neill (*dead*), Jack Fitz[gerald] and his brother, Seán Curtin from Bantry, but now in Cork.[8] Conny Casey, Flyer [Nyhan], Mick [O']Neill and I met Gearóid O'Sullivan and Mick Collins and he told us to get ready.[9] He couldn't say anything about the Treaty as we didn't know much about it. 'What was good enough for me should be good enough for you,' said Collins to us. Collins, Gearóid, and Seán Ó Muirthile used to stay in my place at **[104L]** Christmas from 1917 on, before things got too hot.[10] Seán Donovan was also from Clon(akilty) and he was in the [Wormwood] Scrubs also.[11] We stopped at Boland's (EOM: *Harry Boland's?*). Breen and Treacy were there and they had guns under their pillow.[12]

I was at the camp at Glandore when the IRB was organised. That was in [August 1919].[13] Seán McMahon lectured in

8   These men were all active Cork No. 3 Brigade Volunteers. Crowley, O'Neill and the Fitzgeralds all hailed from Kilbrittain.

9   Gearóid O'Sullivan was adjutant-general of the IRA during the War of Independence, a position he also served with the National Army during the Civil War.

10   Seán Ó Muirthile was a top figure in the IRB. In the Civil War he served as quartermaster general in the National Army with the rank of lieutenant general.

11   It is unclear which Seán Donovan is being talked about as there were a number of Seán/John Donovan/O'Donovans in the area.

12   Dan Breen and Seán Treacy (not Tracey as in the original text) were active IRA leaders from Tipperary.

13   An officers' training camp was held in Glandore during August 1919, organised by Dick McKee, Gearóid O'Sullivan, Leo Henderson and other leaders in the Irish Volunteer organisation.

Engineering.[14] Joe O'Reilly was down there, and Dick McKee and Leo Henderson, Diarmuid O'Hegarty and Seán Ó Muirthile.[15] I had been Captain of Clonakilty Company. Then I was on the Brigade transport until the fighting started. Michael Collins after the Treaty was signed came to Clon[akilty] one night. He sent for a few of us and he offered us anything we could want – positions or money if we would go his way. We told him that we believed in principle and not in jobs. Flyer [Nyhan], Jacky [O']Neill, Mick Crowley were there that night.[16] Mick [Collins] was by himself. He got very stiff then and he made as if to draw his gun. 'Don't mind your gun, Mick,' said Jacky Neill, 'you might have pulled it once when it was needed but you didn't.' Once when I brought up dispatches to Vaughan's [Hotel] in the Tan War I heard Tom Cullen crying for Collins had abused **[105R]** him so much.[17]

14   Seán McMahon (not John MacMahon as in the original text) was a senior figure in the IRB, served as quartermaster in the IRA's GHQ during the War of Independence and succeeded Richard Mulcahy as National Army chief of staff in 1922.

15   Joe O'Reilly, not Reilly as in the original text, was a close aide of Michael Collins; Dick McKee, commander of the IRA's Dublin Brigade, was killed in British custody on 'Bloody Sunday' 1920; Leo Henderson was a senior officer in the Dublin Brigade who served in the anti-Treaty IRA GHQ in the Four Courts during 1922; Diarmuid O'Hegarty was a senior leader of both the military and political wings of the independence movement – the original incorrectly spells this Diurmuid.

16   Jack O'Neill was one of the O'Neill brothers of Kilbrittain; Mick Crowley, also of Kilbrittain, commanded a column in West Cork during the Civil War.

17   Vaughan's Hotel in Parnell Square, Dublin, served as Michael Collins' unofficial headquarters. Tom Cullen was closely associated with Collins' Intelligence Department. During the Civil War he was a major-general in the National Army.

The North: A crowd were picked from the Division to go up North, and we went to Beggar's Bush for a fortnight or 3 weeks. A convoy came for stuff to Moore Park or Mallow, and 4 of us went from Bandon. Dick Willis was picked as a Thompson gunner and Tom Lane from Clonakilty (*dead*).[18] They wanted some from North Cork and from Kerry also. The idea was to tackle Derry city. The Northern Divisional Staff was arrested then. The convoy took up all the machine gun stuff nearly that was in the Division. We got 2 motorbikes to bring back to the Division and on the way back we met [Dinny] Lacey, Packy Dalton (EOM: *In B[eggar's]B[ush] or in Clonmel?*).[19] Dinny Lacey told us to go quickly as they were going to raid the RIC barracks in Clonmel.[20] But the Northern Staff was released then. Gearóid said, 'You go back again.' There were about 40 of us altogether. Theo Fitz (EOM: *?*) was quartermaster general and we were getting uniforms and Gearóid said to him, 'Why don't you give them uniforms according to their rank?'[21] I noticed that all the Dublin men who were in Ballykinlar with me went Free State, for I met

18   Richard 'Dick' Willis was a noted officer from Mallow, North Cork; Tom Lane was an active Volunteer from Clonakilty.

19   Patrick 'Packy' Dalton was O/C of the anti-Treaty 5th Battalion, 3rd Tipperary Brigade and commander of the military barracks at Clonmel.

20   Denis 'Dinny' Lacey was a prominent flying column commander and O/C of the 3rd Tipperary Brigade. He was killed leading Republican forces during the Civil War.

21   Theo Fitzgerald fought in the Easter Rising with Na Fianna and later became an officer in the National Army. Quartermaster general is shortened to QMG in the original text.

them in the Bush.[22] Dan Brophy was there. Later he was in Kerry and he was bad, they said.[23]

Civil War: I went to Tipperary with Jim Hurley and on to Cashel by lorry, and then to Thurles which was to be attacked, but all our columns around Thurles were rounded up but ours, for the others had not put out scouts.[24] Then we were told to attack Golden around 6.[25] The firing stopped and when I **[105L]** was going up a lane I saw caps behind the wall. 'We're in the wrong shop,' I said to Jim Hurley, 'these are [Free] Staters and I'm going.' So I went away but the others, 6 to 8 of them, walked into it. We didn't know then that the rest of our fellows in that attack had retired but they never sent us a word. Then we knocked around a bit, on through Kilkenny to (EOM: *Waterford?*). The rest from the N[orth]. We had between 20 to 30 in our column then. We went in Ballincollig Barracks the night it was being burned, for we had come back through Blarney and then we went back to …[26] We were around for a good while after that. Barry had 100 men. Those men joined us. The Free State were mostly from Skib(bereen), and it was only there that any of the old column

22 Beggar's Bush Barracks. Free State is written as F/S here and elsewhere in the original text.
23 Dan Brophy, O/C of the Fingal Brigade in 1921, was a colonel in the National Army during the Civil War.
24 Jim Hurley was a senior officer in the Cork No. 3 Brigade and a Cork hurling legend who later became bursar of University College Cork.
25 This seems to have occurred around 15 July 1922, during extensive fighting in the area.
26 This occurred on 10 August 1922.

joined them. Father Duggan used to come out to join them.[27] The Staters were afraid of us. Pete Kearney was put in charge of the column there when Tom Barry went up to Tipp[erary].[28] Flyer [Nyhan], Tom Lane, Mick Crowley, Sonny O'Neill left for Glengarriff to go off with Barry; also, Dinny Callaghan and Jack Hennessy of Ballineen were with them: and they were away until about after Christmas.[29] The Staters wouldn't come out, but in **[106R]** a big round up Dan Holland and … were arrested. We were to get the armoured car and he was to raid at Belmont near Upton. Tommy Kelleher, Dan Holland and I went in at 11 o'clock for food and there were supposed to be sentries posted around.[30]

McPeake:[31] Tommy Kennedy has a farm around Upton,

27   Archdeacon Thomas Duggan, commonly referred to as 'Canon Duggan' by contemporaries, was a Republican cleric supportive of the IRA from 1919 to 1921. He also distinguished himself on the battlefield as a British Army chaplain in both the First and Second World Wars.

28   Pete Kearney, a UCC student prominent in the Cork No. 3 Brigade flying column, commanded the Dunmanway Battalion, Cork No. 3 Brigade, during the Civil War.

29   Sonny O'Neill, incorrectly spelled Neale in the original text, was one of the O'Neills of Kilbrittain. He served in the British Army during the First World War and commanded a flying column in the Civil War. The other men mentioned were prominent fighters from West Cork closely associated with Tom Barry. John 'Flyer' Nyhan and Tom Lane came from Clonakilty; Mick Crowley was from Kilbrittain; Denis 'Dinny' Callaghan was an active Volunteer from Newcestown, West Cork; Jack Hennessy of Ballineen served in numerous actions with the Cork No. 3 flying column, including the Kilmichael Ambush.

30   Tom Kelleher and Dan Holland were active West Cork officers closely associated with Tom Barry.

31   John 'Jock' McPeake, incorrectly spelled McPeak in the original text, was a Scotsman born to Irish immigrants in Glasgow. He served in the British

and had intended to give us the armoured car there. The three of us were rounded up. We were from 3 o'clock until dark in the house we were in fighting. Then they sent for a big gun to blow us out of it. It was a thatched house and at the N[orth] end they were setting fire to it. (EOM: *Afterwards McPeake and I met in Glasgow. The day Collins was shot he fired to kill he told me, but later on he found out that the good lads were on our side and so he wanted to hand over the armoured car.*[32] *One fellow in the Joy would have me bowled over for he had his rifle up, only for another who stopped him. We used to call them refugees. Then they weren't good for anything.*) In Belmont when they took us, they brought us on to Bandon.[33] A few of them had been killed in that scrap but we were brought to the officers' mess, where we got a good time. We may thank the Skibbereen men there who had been in the IRA. The day Seán Hales was buried some officer came in to Cork Gaol for a court martial, and we were brought out to the Governor's office.[34] Execution was a matter of form if you were captured with arms (EOM: *or at least the death sentence was*). The officer we had captured in Ballineen

Army during the First World War and after his discharge was jailed for smuggling guns for the IRA in 1921. McPeake was the gunner in the Sliabh na mBan (then called the Slievenamon) armoured car during the Béal na mBláth Ambush in which Michael Collins was killed in August 1922. He deserted to the IRA in December 1922, but was arrested in Glasgow and served a five-year prison sentence in Portlaoise. Following his release he returned to Scotland.

32   Armoured car is written as a/car in the original text.
33   No record could be found of when this took place.
34   The date of his burial was 13 December 1922.

was in charge, and he was in charge of the escort that day that we got court-martialled.[35] The day we captured him we **[106L]** had given him a good time. They took us to the Governor's office and he was then sent away on escort. He said to us, 'if you have any friends at headquarters get them to do something for they mean to shoot you.'

'We don't want favours,' we said to him.

Neilus Connolly and the Skib[bereen] crowd, when they heard that Tommy and I were to be executed they went up to Cork to see Ennis, and they said that if anything happened to us there would be no Free State Army in West Cork.[36] We were brought out in the yard each day. Seán Buckley from Bandon was there and he spoke Irish, and a convict who was there spoke to him in Irish, and he said, 'they're digging a grave out at the back today'. The lads outside sent notices around the country that if anything was to happen to us all the Unionists in the county would be shot and the Staters' places were to be burned, and prominent ones shot. The Skib[bereen] crowd really saved us, for most everyone who was in the IRA had joined up the Free State there.

35   In charge is written as i/c in the original text, here and elsewhere. Ballineen is incorrectly spelled Ballyneen in the original text.

36   Cornelius 'Neilus' Connolly commanded the Skibbereen Battalion of the Cork No. 3 Brigade during the War of Independence. He and most of his officers went pro-Treaty during the Civil War. Connolly represented the West Cork constituency in Dáil Éireann from 1922 to 1927. Major-General Tom Ennis, a top figure in the Dublin Brigade during the War of Independence, became a senior commander of the National Army in Munster during the Civil War.

Joe Mac... and the officers came up in lorries and they saw Tom Ennis.[37] He wasn't for this execution, he said, but he would have to do his duty and he might have to do for them. **[107R]** He would do his duty, he said, but he'd get in touch with GHQ about them. They told him to wireless to Dublin. Poor Flyer [Nyhan] was punished after the 'Ceasefire'.[38] They brought 8 murder charges against them, but he and Tom Lane were sent on to Hare Park.[39] Gearóid [O'Sullivan] when he was passing through went to see Flyer's people. He wouldn't do anything for Flyer, he said, for Flyer was then being tried, and even if he was guilty I would not save him. And Gearóid was very friendly always with Flyer's people.

We were sent to the Joy from Cork Gaol in April or in June. We were in the female gaol in Cork. There was an old sewer under the gaol and as I was quartermaster of the squad who had to be down there every night, I had to be there also.[40] The Free Staters would come in at night but they wouldn't look at the

37   It is unclear who is meant by Joe Mac.
38   The Irish Civil War ended when the IRA called a ceasefire at the end of April 1923, which was followed in May 1923 with an order to 'dump arms'.
39   In March 1924, John 'Flyer' Nyhan was charged with the murder of RIC District Inspector Kenny (11 February 1922), Army Volunteer Michael MacDonald (26 December 1922) and Postmaster Jerome Reilly (25 or 26 January 1923). Tom Lane was charged with the same killings, as well as the murder of civilian Robert Nagle, one of thirteen Protestant civilian victims to die during the controversial 'Bandon Valley killings' of April 1922. See Bielenberg, Borgonovo and Donnelly (2014). Hare Park was one of two internment camps for Civil War prisoners located in the Curragh. The Tintown camps made up the other.
40   He is referring to tunnelling out of the prison.

cells, but the sentry would walk up and down the ground floor for a time. The lads used to be down in the sewer in the daytime also. There was a civilian plumber who came into the gaol to do jobs, and he used to bring us in hacksaw blades which were nearly 2 inches square. Someone gave the game away, but they were in searching for a week before they found our way down to the sewer. Jack Fitzgerald, Connie Casey, Seán McCarthy, Dick Willis were there, and they were all on the left hand side of the … wing as you go in to the gaol.[41]

The night we came into the Joy we were put out into the yard and we got back in the morning sometime. Fitzpatrick, the Deputy Governor, came down to me while I was on hunger strike, and he said, 'You're foolish to go on **[107L]** hunger strike.'

'You didn't say that once, I know,' I answered.

'How so?' he asked.

'When you were in the Scrubs we were on hunger strike and you approved of it then.'

After that he was very kind to me. There was ice in the water in the Joy in the morning. I was up every day during the strike, but Johnny Connors stayed in bed most of the time and

---

41   These were all prominent IRA officers. Jack Fitzgerald's interview comes later in this volume; Con Casey of Tralee served with the Kerry No. 1 Brigade and later as a 1st Southern Division organiser; Dick Willis was an active fighter in the Cork No. 2 Brigade; Seán McCarthy, incorrectly spelled MacCarthy in the original, served on the 1st Southern Division staff and was later a president of the GAA.

rested.[42] The windows were broken in the cell and we heated water on the gas.

Jack Fitz[gerald] and Liam Deasy from our area finished it out. There were not many on it when the strike was over. Frank Barrett was with us in Cork Gaol and Todd Andrews also.[43]

Peace moves: Seán McCarthy, Joe Kearney, a brother of Peter, and Tommy Reidy went on a peace move, and they had a good time when they were out of gaol.[44] We were in Cork Gaol one day sitting down in our cells and we heard Raymond Kennedy rapping on his cell door.[45] 'Sentry I want to go to the lavatory please,' but there was no reply. 'Open the f— door,' we shouted, and the door was opened at once. 'Talk to them,' we said, 'in their own language, not in convenient language.' Mick [O']Neill and Bert Norrey (EOM: *from Muhally's column*)[46] were in the **[108R]** time we were in the Joy. Then we were moved to Hare Park. We were on a tunnel there when we were only a short time in the camp. Flyer and I were on one section. This went out from one of the huts, a

---

42 No information could be found on Johnny Connors.
43 Frank Barrett of Mid-Clare served on the IRA Executive; Dubliner Todd Andrews, incorrectly spelled Tod in the original, acted as Liam Lynch's staff officer until the latter's death.
44 Joe Kearney was an active member of the University College Cork section of the IRA; Tom Reidy was Cork No. 5 Brigade intelligence officer.
45 Raymond Kennedy, a staff officer with the Cork No. 1 Brigade during the War of Independence and Civil War, was a chemistry lecturer at University College Cork during and after his war service.
46 This is probably a reference to Patrick Mullaney, who operated the Kildare/Meath column from the autumn of 1922 until it was captured (twenty-two men) with weapons at the beginning of December 1922.

small hut. It was just started when it was caught. The Staters came in fairly quick and they found the tunnel, for we were only just up out of it. We were told to get out quick before the Staters came.

J. O'Connor, solicitor in Tralee. There was poteen made in the [prison] cookhouse out of spuds. (EOM: *They never make poteen in Kerry, I am told.*) Kealkil was a great place for the making of the poteen. Liam O'Dwyer and the local fellows kept the British going.[47] The Bantry fellows went back then to the Beara Peninsula. Seán [O']Driscoll in Ballydehob was a good fellow. He came in with Seán Lehane to the column after Tom Barry got sick.[48]

Chess: Liam Deasy used to play chess in our hut. Spud Murphy is a preventative officer in Dundalk.[49] He was from Clon(akilty) and he was on the column from the start to the finish and indeed he used to be too careful. He was very fond of the poteen and the drink.

47   Liam O'Dwyer was O/C of the Castletownbere Battalion, Cork No. 5 Brigade.
48   Seán O'Driscoll was an active member of Cork No. 3 Brigade during the War of Independence. Seán Lehane assumed temporary command of the brigade flying column, following Tom Barry's hospitalisation in December 1920.
49   James 'Spud' Murphy of Clonakilty was a very active member of the Cork No. 3 Brigade who participated in numerous attacks and ambushes.

BILLY O'SULLIVAN

(UCDA P17b/111, pp. 46–48)

A native of Bantry, William 'Billy' O'Sullivan (?–1957) served with the British Army in the First World War. The former Munster Fusilier became a valued member of the Cork No. 3 Brigade flying column during the War of Independence, owing to his expertise with a Lewis gun. Among his combat actions was the daring machine-gun attack on British soldiers playing football in Bandon during May 1921, under the command of Tom Barry. He fought with the Republican forces during the Civil War. During the Second World War he returned to military life, and trained National Army recruits at Collins Barracks in Cork. O'Sullivan lived in Bantry at the time of his death in 1957. He was survived by his wife and three children.

***

[46R] I went up North with Seán Lehane and Mossy Donegan,[1]

---

1   Seán Lehane, Cork No. 3 Brigade, commanded the Schull area and flying columns in 1920 and 1921. He succeeded Liam Deasy as brigade commander during the Truce period, but resigned his position when Tom Hales was released from prison. In the Civil War, Lehane commanded Republican forces in Ulster during the border offensive. For Mossy Donegan, see his interview.

and we had Divisional headquarters in Raphoe.[2] Charlie Daly was there.[3] I think Lehane was up before us and he came back for us. Then Seán began to organise. Mossy Donegan was brigade O/C, I was O/C Training on the Divisional Staff. In March [1922] the local Orangemen would signal when we were moving out from our Divisional headquarters.[4] Peadar O'Donnell was a Brigade O/C too (Peadar was shifted from the Curragh a few days before we escaped).[5]

We went in across the border between Lifford and Johnstown. We went in about 2 miles and attacked a big outpost of [B] Specials, about 120, in a camp where there also were soldiers. Mossy Donegan was there with half the column, Charlie Daly, Seán Lehane and Frank O'Donnell.[6] We attacked the lights in the camp and we billeted. Every man had to do his stuff. We came back to the outskirts of

---

2   Raphoe is in County Donegal.
3   Charlie Daly, senior IRA officer active in Kerry and Dublin, commanded the 2nd Northern Division during the 1922 Ulster campaign. He was executed by the National Army at Drumboe Castle in March 1923.
4   Headquarters is written as Hd Qrs in the original text.
5   Peadar O'Donnell from Meenmore in Donegal was a noted Republican socialist. He was active in the northern counties during the War of Independence and was strongly opposed to the Anglo-Irish Treaty, becoming a member of the anti-Treaty IRA Executive. Captured in the Four Courts in 1922, he was imprisoned for the duration of the Civil War. He was involved in the digging of the tunnel in the Curragh through which O'Sullivan escaped, but was moved to Mountjoy before the escape attempt took place. He was held in various jails throughout his incarceration, but eventually escaped from the Curragh in March 1924.
6   Frank O'Donnell was the brother of Peadar O'Donnell.

Newtown Cunningham. We thought Joe Sweeney and Co. would reinforce us.[7]

Billy Holmes was a Free State captain in charge of the barracks in Raphoe.[8] We had the Masonic Hall there. We had Finner Camp and troops out in Stoney's.[9] We came back that night and were forming up the column in Newtown Cunningham when 5 or 6 lorries of Staters came in, and they let bang, and we let bang and we took them prisoners. We handed them over. Joe Sweeney was going to declare war on us.[10]

Johnstown: The Protestant element cleared out when they heard the Catholics were coming. They were made to take down 'to Hell with the Pope'. The Catholics had run out because **[46L]** they thought the Protestants were coming. We blew up the petrol tanks that night on the outskirts of the village.

British soldiers came for a drink and our fellows on Lifford Bridge …

We attacked this side of Strabane, a patrol, but we didn't know what happened.

Billy Pilkington's troops were in Pettigo and the British

7   Major-General Joseph Sweeney, O/C of the West Donegal (No. 1) Brigade in the War of Independence, was GOC of the National Army in County Donegal during the Civil War and a TD in Dáil Éireann.
8   Free State is written as F/S and in charge is written as i/c in the original text.
9   Finner Camp was a former British Army base at Ballyshannon, County Donegal. It is not known what Stoney's refers to.
10   Sweeney, not MacSweeney as in the original text.

shelled it.[11] I was there that night after the Br[itish] had shelled it. Some of our men out of Bundoran ran out for reinforcements for them.

Lifford Bridge: 3 [British soldiers] came over unarmed, and our fellows kept them in Lifford Barracks but one of our own officers let them out. They only wandered across the bridge.

I was arrested on the 2nd day of July [1922], brought from Raphoe to Drumboe, when I was asked to come over.[12] Then from Buncrana I was brought on a boat, the *Helga*, to Mountjoy, and from there I was shifted to the Curragh with Peadar [O'Donnell] on the 28th of December.[13] I was in 'A' Wing with Gerry Boland.[14] Andy Mac was in charge of the wing.[15] There was an Errigal man, one of the Connaughts, attached to the Dublin Brigade there also.[16] I had been in **[47R]** the

---

11   This refers to the 'Pettigo Incident', a week-long clash along the Northern Ireland border between British and pro-Treaty troops in late May to early June 1922. William 'Billy' or 'Liam' Pilkington of Sligo was O/C of the 3rd Western Division during the Civil War. He subsequently joined the priesthood.

12   He may have been asked to defect to the National Army.

13   During the 1916 Easter Rising, the Royal Navy's armed yacht *Helga* shelled Dublin city centre and she was used by the Free State government during the Civil War. Eventually renamed *Muirchu*, she was later used for fishery protection duties.

14   Gerald 'Gerry' Boland, not Jerrie as in the original text, was the brother of Harry Boland. He was active with the anti-Treaty forces in the Civil War and a senior figure in Fianna Fáil during his thirty-eight years in Dáil Éireann.

15   Andy, not Andie as in the original text, McDonnell was O/C of the Dublin No. 2 (South County Dublin) Brigade.

16   The Connaught Rangers was a British Army regiment raised in the province of Connaught.

fourth battalion of the Munsters.[17] Brian O'Higgins and I were in the one cell, 17-A-3.[18] I plonked one of the revolvers in the lavatory at the lower end on the morning of the scrap.[19]

There was a tunnel going to the Rug Factory from A Wing which was caught a few nights before we could get out.

End April [1923], Tin Town 3. Sonny Sullivan of Listowel, Patsy Clifford, and ... Price, all three Kerrymen.[20] O'Callaghan of Limerick, Micky Reid of Howth who has a big shop on the Main St[reet] there now. The tunnel was in my hut. There was a concrete floor and we cut a slab. A light would remain lighting below in the tunnel so they stole the electric light wire out of the chapel and connected up the lights. And there we plonked the stuff we got out of the tunnel. Mick Howlett, Waterford, wasn't on it. Mick Devane, Tralee, the manager of the Exchange [Hotel] was on it but he didn't escape.[21] I was the 23rd man out of the tunnel. The flag inside the door was lifted and I am sure the shaft was sunk at least 10 feet, for it was in sandy ground it was and the shape of it had to be egg shaped (EOM: *for support*), and it went out under the road. We kept fellows from playing football near one hut for the clay would fall down from

17   The Munster Fusiliers was a British Army regiment raised in the province of Munster.
18   Brian O'Higgins was a Republican activist, TD, writer and publisher of the *Wolfe Tone Annual*.
19   There is no information on what scrap he is talking about.
20   Patsy Clifford was one of the Kerry Volunteers dispatched to Ulster during the Truce period.
21   No information could be found on Howlett or Devane.

the sheeting boards (EOM: *if the ball bounced off the outside wall*) and from the corrugated iron. We would go out to try and meet the football. There were only 3 huts in our camp, and 100 in each hut, and only one hut knew of the tunnel. Peadar O'Donnell was O/C of our hut and we were to escape on a Thursday **[47L]** night. I was in charge of No. 3 section for 11 men were to escape at a time, 10 men and a leader. We had a big ball of twine to the mouth of the tunnel, and the last man out would pull the twine to tell the men at the head of the tunnel that they could now go ahead as the tunnel was clear. On Thursday we were to escape, and on Tuesday, Peadar was taken away and we were afraid the game was up, so we waited for Saturday night. Tommy Reidy went out [and] got to the mouth of the tunnel and cut the barbed wire in the camp.[22] He pulled the string when he was ready to get away. Peadar was the leading light there and the Free Staters were watching Peadar. The alarm often went in the Curragh for the sentries often got the wind up (EOM: *and I suppose they had been screwed up by the threats of their officers*) and the Staters would swarm into the camp and search the huts. The racehorses would break out of their stables in Brownstown every now and then. I told my group we're not going far, for if we do get out we don't know where to go. I went less than a mile where we lay in the furze. There was a main road outside and we didn't know it was a main road till we saw the lorries on it.

22   Tom Reidy was Cork No. 5 Brigade's intelligence officer.

[48R] Five of us left: Micky Reidy, Sonny Sullivan to bring men to Naas to get in touch with the Dublin people.[23] That evening we could see troops coming along in skirmish order a half a mile away and we [heard] the 'fall in' whistle then. I waited for the night and I'll never forget it. There was a woman who had a cake in the oven and we asked her for a bit of bread. She said, 'You're some of the escapees' and she gave us the whole cake. 'You can see the Wicklow Mountains from here,' she said. Before the escape I knew that a certain number of us was to get out so I was always taking bearings. Two of us went up to a lodge-keeper's house. There was a foxy woman there. I knocked and I asked if she could help a poor man. 'Come in me darlin',' she said, 'you're some of the escaped prisoners.' We all came in to eat but yet we were afraid of them, even though they swore to us that they were Republicans. The husband had a niece who was also niece to Conor Murphy of Tinahely, and he went to find her.[24] Coming on morning we went with the niece to Tinahely and we went into a big house, a Free Stater's house, brought there by the niece; and the Free Staters came into the pub below to drink. The house was afraid of the Canon, that he'd catch us there, and after 29 days I arrived at last at Kealkil. I had had an awful time from Prout, for I

23   Sonny Sullivan was an active IRA officer in the Bantry area. No information could be found on Micky Reidy.
24   Tinahely, County Wexford, not Tinahealy as in the original text. No information could be found on Conor Murphy.

found it hard to get through Waterford.[25] Mick Reidy left us in Tinahely.

In the Camp, the Free Staters would come in to search the camp. Major MacDonnell was O/C [of] the camp. They'd tap away for tunnels. We burned the fibre in our mattresses to make room for [48L] the earth. You could leave a man from another hut inside for you'd take him out again. Fellows who were brought in at that time got an awful doing for this was the last push off.

[Ted] O'Sullivan. In … we had two dugouts well built. The Staters tied laurel on Ted's head and they beat him in the street, but Ettie Walsh, a fish woman, put her arms around him to protect him.[26] They were all strangers, she said, though she knew him and his people well and all about him. [O']Friel, who beat up Ted, travels for Cork Distilleries.[27]

Captain Shanley shot himself at Una Foley Lodge.[28] He was an intelligence officer on Collins' intelligence staff.[29] Ned Cotter was a prisoner with Ted that day.[30]

---

25   Major-General John T. Prout commanded the National Army troops in Waterford.
26   For additional information on Ted O'Sullivan's torture, see his interview.
27   Commandant Frank O'Friel of the National Army.
28   Captain John 'Jack' Shanley died of a self-inflicted gunshot wound while posted in Bantry during January 1924.
29   Intelligence officer is written I/O in the original text.
30   Edward 'Ned' Cotter was a veteran Republican from Bantry, who held the West Cork seat for Fianna Fáil from 1945 to 1967.

JACK FITZGERALD

(UCDA P17b/112, pp. 91–103)

Jack Fitzgerald (?–1977) was born into a noted Republican farming family in Kilbrittain. He participated in numerous actions with the famous Kilbrittain Company, until his capture in October 1920. During the Civil War he was sent to the north with other Cork officers, and took command of the 4th Donegal Brigade. He was later captured and imprisoned in the south. In later years he joined Old IRA committees and participated in various funeral firing parties. He lived out his days in Clashareague, Kilbrittain, dying in 1977.

***

[91R] **Granassig:** Percival's column stayed there for a week.[1] There were 150 men, 2 lorries, a company of 4 platoons. They

---

1   Granassig is near Kilbrittain. Major Edward Percival, intelligence officer with the 1st Battalion, Essex Regiment, was stationed in Bandon from 1920 to 1922. In 1921 he operated his own mobile column in West Cork to harass the IRA. During the Second World War, Lt General Percival surrendered Singapore to the Japanese, suffering one of the worst defeats in British history.

bought potatoes locally. They stayed in [O']Reilly's for a week, a half a mile from the sea it was. One of the boys from that house was killed in the Bandon Barracks attack.[2] Kinsale was then in the 1st [Cork] Brigade (IRA) instead of being with Cork 3 [Brigade].

Excommunication:[3] This affected the 4th and 5th battalions.[4] We were the 1st Battalion (EOM: *which Deasy says was the best battalion in Ireland*). In Schull and in the country further west, Seán Lehane said that it affected 50% of his men. It had no effect on this [Kilbrittain] area. This battalion had 10–11 companies, A–H: Ballinadee, Timoleague, Quarry Cross, Inishannon, Ballinspittle, Barryroe, Bandon, Kilbrittain.[5] [Mick] Crowley is from this area, Newcestown, Upton.[6]

In Kilbrittain we captured 5 rifles by disarming a patrol.[7] We had a .32 [calibre] revolver. There were 5 soldiers and a policeman for they didn't stir out there without a policeman. He was their intelligence officer and a guide. We would only be allowed to shoot a bad RIC man, and then he might not be the

2   Volunteer Daniel O'Reilly was killed in action at Bandon on 24 January 1921, when Cork No. 3 Brigade forces attempted to attack a military curfew patrol operating from the barracks.
3   Excommunication edict issued against active IRA members by Catholic Bishop Daniel Cohalan of the Cork diocese in December 1920.
4   Cohalan's Cork diocese only covered part of the Cork No. 3 Brigade area.
5   Some of these names are misspelled in the original and have been corrected here.
6   Mick Crowley commanded a column in West Cork during the Civil War.
7   On 16 June 1919 fourteen Volunteers of Kilbrittain Company (all but two unarmed) ambushed a military patrol at Rathclarin and disarmed the five soldiers and one RIC constable.

real source of information. Take the case of Sergeant Cornelius Crean, who was the most diplomatic man that ever walked.[8] Yet he was one of their head intelligence men. He would say, 'God Bless you', and 'God Bless the work', as he passed by, or he'd stop to chat lightly and easily. 'Were you in such a place last night?' would maybe be his next question. He was shot in an ambush in Inishannon.

Evacuated Barracks: Ballinspittle: south of the river.

Courtmacsherry.

We attacked Timoleague Barracks but the RIC did not **[92R]** evacuate. Bandon was a battalion headquarters for the British.[9] We attacked Kilbrittain Barracks 3 times but the explosives always failed. That was a pity. We had guncotton, enough of it indeed to blow up the village. We placed the charge against the wall on two occasions, and we went under and through the barbed wire which was protecting the gable ends, but the explosive always failed. It might be the detonators that were at fault.

In 1920 the only armed Coast Guard Station (CGS) was at Howe's Strand. We attacked it the first time, but there the coast guards were not armed or maybe had only 4 or 5 rifles. Then we made an attack on the 10th of May,[10] when we captured ten

8   This name is misspelled as Crehan Crene in the original text. The RIC sergeant was shot dead by the IRA on 25 April 1920. He was the brother of noted Polar explorer Tom Crean.
9   Battalion headquarters is written as Bn Hd Qrs in the original text.
10   O'Malley has inserted a note above '10th of May' to say *this was the first*.

rifles.[11] The two last raids were in June and July. Charlie Hurley was a member of this company, then he became Brigade O/C. So in this last attack Charlie carried in other companies to make it a success, so that in all our CGS captures were 5 + 10 + 14 = 29 rifles. Charlie Hurley got 5 years for carrying documents in Castletownbere.[12] He was released under the Cat and Mouse Act, and was supposed to report to his local RIC barracks once a month, but he didn't.[13]

The Protestants were very strong here but they were not a bad crowd at all mind you, and none of them were shot as spies as happened in other places in the brigade.

Spies: See Tom Barry's book about that.

In the first attack on the CGS we captured boxes of ammunition and equipment, and on the second attack we got a lot of ammo also. There was a big wireless set there, which was put up by us in our area but it was not effective.

[92L] Tapping of wires: We tapped wires later on, but we didn't get anything out of it.

---

11   Fitzgerald appears to have his dates wrong. The IRA captured Howe's Strand coastguard station (near Kilbrittain) twice, on 22 June and 22 July 1920. It is unclear exactly how many rifles they seized, though Fitzgerald's figure of ten and fourteen appears roughly correct.

12   Charlie Hurley was a member of the Irish Volunteers from a young age. He was also an active member of Sinn Féin, the GAA and the Gaelic League. He commanded Cork No. 3 Brigade from 1920, after the capture of Tom Hales, until his death on 19 March 1921, when he was shot by British soldiers at Ballinphellic, near Upton in County Cork.

13   The Cat and Mouse Act, introduced by the Asquith government, allowed prisoners on hunger strike to be released for reasons of ill-health and imprisoned again once they were recovered.

The Column: There was a man in it at first, from every company in the battalion, then afterwards there were 10 men from our company in the Brigade Column, and for any major fight our men would be called in. There were a lot of men on the run who could be called upon when necessary.

October 1920: I was captured a mile from here [Clashareague, Kilbrittain]. I left this house for I had been out with the column and I came home for a change of clothes. I chatted away with my first cousin, who was back from the USA, and then I went into bed. And in about a quarter of an hour I heard a noise of lorries. Mick [O']Neill was with me.[14] We jumped out of bed. He was in his shirt and I had my pants in my hand. They opened fire on us and we were under their fire for a mile. When I got down the lane I put on my trousers, but they cornered us. A few soldiers were running after us but we were covered with a rifle. It was the Kinsale crowd, the Essex, who had captured us. It looked very much like as if we had been given away.

I had been at the training camps at that time. We had been to the west on **[93R]** the Dunmanway road for a week. Then we ran into an ambush in Newcestown. We billeted in the battalion. The [1st Battalion] O/C Seán Hales went up to the north to find out how things were there, and whilst he was

---

14   Michael O'Neill, an O'Neill brother of Kilbrittain, was acting commander of the 1st Battalion, Cork No. 3 Brigade, at the time of his death in Ballygroman, County Cork, in April 1922.

there 2 lorries of the British came on him, and he got out of it and he took us back up to the village.[15] Two lorries came into us while we were coming out of the village. We jumped inside a fence and we opened up on them, and we blazed away at each other. It was pitch dark, but they threw themselves out and they outflanked us and they had to retreat. The officer was killed and several of the soldiers as they tried to flank us.[16] We were there after 2 weeks training, so we decided to go out and to look for an ambush under the lads who had been trained. Half of our men were not in this fight, only the first lot of us who [were] up there. We tried to reorganise and surround them again. Next morning we found a soldier's tunic in the middle of the field and a ten shilling note inside it.[17] It had been put there so that their wounded officer could rest on [it]. We were to have held the next camp in Newcestown, but the ambush knocked out that idea, so we were to shift to Ballymurphy in the east, and we waited for the British to come back to reprisal [*sic*], but they didn't come then. They came later and they burned a few houses around the place. Then we went under [Tom] Barry to Ballymurphy for a week, and he gave us an awful time of it. And that training went on within a mile of an RIC barracks in Kilbrittain. The training was carried on quite openly: now weren't the people great. The British came [93L] within a mile

15   Hales had been surprised by two British lorries, but escaped and redeployed his men to evade the threat.
16   The fight at Newcestown occurred on 9 October 1920.
17   Ten shilling is written as 10/s in the original text.

of us one night and they arrested a man, and the next day they murdered him a mile outside the town. He was an Irish Volunteer. The British here were very bad for you couldn't be safe with them, but they never even insulted me when they had me. We stayed a week in Ballymurphy, then we lay out on the Cork–Bandon road. A lorry didn't pass that whole day for they knew that we were there. We had from 60 to 70 men for the attack. We lay there all day and at dark we were disbanded for 2 days and then we were to come back to the same road again.

Two soldiers marched us with our hands up. Mick was in his shirt. We were taken to Bandon, but first we were brought back and allowed to dress and we had our breakfast. Capt[ain] Spooner was a decent officer. We ran because we thought it was all over with us, for Connolly from Bandon, who had gone out to sleep outside, had been murdered the week before we were captured.[18] We were put into a cell; there were 5 to 6 local prisoners inside from the Bally... area, but they were black and blue from the battering they had got. They were sleeping on the flags and they hadn't even a blanket to put under them. We were certain that **[94R]** we should soon see our end, but we protested that we needed something to sleep on and a bundle of 20 blankets were hurled in at once. Both of us were questioned before an interrogating officer. I was captain of the co[mpany],

18   Lt John Connolly of Bandon was arrested by British troops in Kilbrittain on 24 September and taken to Bandon Barracks. His corpse was discovered some time later.

and they said I was captain of the co[mpany], and also stated that I was in Newcestown on the ambush the week before. Spooner was present during this interrogation. He knew whilst we were in Bandon that the ambush that was planned next day for the Cork–Bandon road would be brought off and we were told that we would be removed. We knew what would most certainly happen to us if we were kept in Bandon when the ambush came off. But we were moved, 12 of us, but [O']Neill and I were put in with a lorry of Tans. Tom Barry, who knew that we had been arrested, postponed the ambush for a day or two. And when we were shifted to Cork we went up the road along which we had lain in ambush a few days before that. The lorries were stopped and the Tans said, 'Ye were here the other day waiting for us. We were lucky not to come here that day.' We were warned now, 'any minute and ye'll be shot dead if your fellows fired a shot' and the Tans kept their rifles pointed at us. On the following day an ambush came off at Toureen.[19] We were brought to the Detention Barracks, Cork, and from a soldier there we heard that there had been an ambush 5 minutes after. All prisoners had been removed from Bandon the night the ambush took place.

We were in the Detention Barracks for from 5 to 6 weeks. The rules there were very strict. We moved around in twos

---

19   On 22 October Cork No. 3 Brigade forces ambushed part of a British military convoy at Toureen, near Ballinhassig on the Bandon road. They killed at least three soldiers and disarmed the rest.

[94L] in the ring for exercise and we had to keep quiet, not talk, and we were only allowed out for an hour or two. There were hundreds of prisoners there, and there was not a hope of escape from it. Outside they were trying to rescue us, but they could not get any inside information that would be of any use to them. We had a warder there who was alright, and he would bring out letters. There were only Mick and I from our area. We were taken before a board of five officers for enquiries. We were given the day before a paper on which there were 10 to 12 questions, and we had been given 24 hours to consider it, and if we didn't answer it we could be sentenced. We decided to answer the questions on the paper.

'Were you a captain of Kilbrittain Company?'

'Do you know Seán Hales Battalion Commandant?'

'Were you in such an attack?'

So I answered, 'I know Seán Hales, he's my first cousin. Why shouldn't I know him?' I said I was an Irish Volunteer.

'Why did you run the morning you were arrested?'

They asked me to sign it. You were put on your oath, but I wouldn't sign it. That proved they knew nothing. They arrested a first cousin of mine a week later. 'They told me they had you,' he said afterwards, 'and that they were [95R] going to make me pay for it'. The Howe's Strand coastguards knew me well for they had seen enough of me, but not one of them came forwards either to identify me or to give evidence against me, and that speaks well for them, and I give them great credit for that. We were brought out on parade on what was really an identification parade and we knew that someone was spying on us. Before Christmas we were put in a boat, a few hundred of us. We were shifted in lorries to the boat in Cork. It was a big cargo boat. We were thrown into it in a heap, and in this way we went by sea to Belfast. The crew were cooking and we were taken on deck for one half hour. I think there were many men aboard. I was not very sick for the weather was calm, but we saw nothing of the country on our way up. We arrived at night, and at night we got through by train to Ballykinlar, and there we walked to the camp.[20] We had a royal time in the camp, to give the British fair play. There were from 25 to 30 in every hut in Camp One. We began a tunnel in April. Mossy Donegan was in another Hut, D, and I was in C.[21] We started the tunnel from inside a hut in a cubicle, which was a little square off the main building. We cut a trap door out of it in the floor, and there was a door on the cubicle also. We began to dig straight away in hard compressed sand. We had little shovels and short roundy spades. We put the material in under the huts (EOM: *it was easy to get rid of, for both the camps were in sand*). The camp was on a sandbank so it wouldn't be noticed, the sand that we got rid of.

[95L] We didn't work at night, yerra we'll do it in the

20   Ballykinlar Internment Camp was opened in late 1920, on the coast of County Down. The Royal Navy often transported Munster prisoners there by warship.
21   For Maurice 'Mossy' Donegan, see his interview.

daytime. There were Br[itish] sentries at the four corners and we had scouts out to watch for the British whenever they would come in for inspection. We could only work at the [tunnel] face one at a time. We had a railway line made of the frame of old houses, which we had torn to pieces.[22] Con Leary from the mountains was the chief tradesman. He is now living in Dublin and he was from Clonakilty: 'Usen't I make all these things,' he said: wooden flanges on the truck which would occupy only the bare breadth of the line, and a siding so that one truck could pass another. We were thinking of putting in electric light. The military when they captured it put it on paper. There were two trucks at the sidings. That was when the distance became long, and the truck held about 5 to 6 buckets of sand. We made use of candles for lighting, but as the tunnel was very narrow we worked in the dark. We put up holes to give us air, for even so it was very close below, and you wouldn't be more than half an hour when you'd be thoroughly exhausted. After about 20 minutes you'd be a body of sweat.

Then we thought we'd find out where we were going, for our intention was to make for a fence, **[96R]** which was from a 100 to 120 yards away, for beyond that was grand cover from the sentries: otherwise it was an open plain. Then either a dispatch sent out to make final arrangements was caught or something we did was spotted inside the camp. The British

22   Carts on tracks, to remove earth.

one day came in to dig all around the camp, and then dug a trench. When we were trying to see if the direction was correct we first put up a little red flag which was about two inches square. An officer and a dog were walking around outside and the dog began to bark. We could hear the officer say, 'Come on you damn fool, what are you barking at there?' The flag showed us that we had been going in the wrong direction, so we cut off in another direction again. We were now 5 or 6 weeks at the tunnel. When the British found out what hut it was from, all members of the hut were taken out of the camp and they were court-martialled, but they were all allowed back from detention after a fortnight. There was a tunnel begun from another hut but I wasn't on it and I knew nothing about it, but the result of this other tunnel was that a 4-ton lorry fell through into it. I had dug to the water level but the engineers so worked it that it went deep at the trench, they … through water. If we had gone another inch we would have had the water. For props we had bed boards, for each man provided one bed board. A good many must have been about the tunnel. The bed boards were six feet by 9 inches. There was a grand spring in them and **[96L]** there was a 2½ foot trestle under them. There was a third tunnel which was found after a short time for it began after the Truce. We were released before the Treaty was ratified, the two camps of us, and we came on to Dublin where Tom Barry gave us a spread and a 'do'. We got a mauling in the train coming down from the Orangemen with bricks, stones and lumps of coal. Then Barry got in touch with Gearóid O'Sullivan, and when we met him one of our lads said to him, 'Are you going to sell the country?'[23]

And Gearóid's reply was, 'And who has a better right to sell it?'

We went to see Collins also but he was drunk. There were 1,000 prisoners and half of them were not Irish Volunteers. They were very g[ood] indeed inside and many of them joined up the Irish Volunteers there.[24]

The British allowed drill to go on in the camp for a couple of months until they stopped it one day. We then had physical drill instead. There was a Scots Regiment guarding us. There were a few different regiments there, and the line officers wore kilts. Tadhg Barry [97R] was shot in No. 2 camp and two lads in our camp No. 1.[25] Sloan and Tormey were both killed with the one bullet.[26] When I got out I had to go to hospital to get dressed. There were in all about 20 of us from West Cork.

---

23 Gearóid O'Sullivan was adjutant-general of the IRA during the War of Independence, a position he also served in the National Army during the Civil War.

24 Irish Volunteers is written as IVs in the original text, both here and elsewhere.

25 Tadhg Barry, misspelled in the original text as Tadg, was a journalist, a pioneer of the independence movement in Cork city and an alderman on Cork Corporation. He was shot on Tuesday 15 November 1921 by a sentry at the camp.

26 Patrick Sloan and Joseph Tormey, both of Moate, County Westmeath, were shot dead by a sentry in Ballykinlar Internment Camp on 17 January 1921. The shot struck Joseph Tormey in the head, passed through him and hit Patrick Sloan in the neck.

In my hut discussion was very much opposed to the [*sic*] any giving way by our negotiators in London.[27] And I think that when they got out, all that hut were Republican. Tracey and Lalor were there and some Clare men.[28] A brigade meeting was held in Bandon. There was no one from the Brigade in favour of it, and Seán Hales was then against the Treaty. Seán was battalion O/C then, and Seán Lehane, who had been out all the time, was brigade O/C. Seán L[ehane] was fierce to the world against this Treaty, and I went back with Seán during the Truce to the West. The Battalion O/C (EOM: *is this Hales?*) pulled only officers with him but no one in this battalion went Free State, and that was a great relief afterwards, for there was no enmity between us. Con Lehane of Timoleague was an officer (EOM: *in the IRB?*).[29]

Seán Lehane, although he need not have done so, resigned his position as Brigade O/C and [Tom] Hales was then brigade O/C. That left Seán L[ehane] a spare part, so in March or April [1922] he went to the North. I was then in Kinsale Barracks. (Jim) Seamus Cotter from [the] North side [of] Ballinhassig,[30] near Kinsale, was battalion quartermaster and then Brigade

---

27   His colleagues opposed concessions in the Anglo-Irish Treaty negotiations then being carried out in London.
28   It is not known who Tracey and Lalor were.
29   Con Lehane was the first commander of the Timoleague Company, in the Bandon Battalion, Cork No. 3 Brigade. A blacksmith, he served as an armourer on the brigade staff.
30   O'Malley likely made a mistake by writing the word 'Noble' in the original text, instead of the more probable 'North'.

O/C of South Donegal. [Jim] Lane was a column O/C in the North at the time.[31] Galvin of Bantry was Div[isional] Transport Officer.[32] Jimmy [O']Sullivan of Bantry, Transport Officer.[33] Tom Mullins: Ass[istant] Div[isional] Adjutant.[34] Charlie Daly: Divisional Vice-Commandant.

[97L] Seán Lehane Divisional O/C: Con Crowley of Kilbrittain was also in the North.[35] There was a swap of rifles for us. We had no Thompsons and no Lewis guns. (EOM: *Indeed, Lewis Guns would have only been of use for stunts, or in the beginning of the Civil War, for their use meant a wastage of ammunition.*)

Raphoe was Divisional Headquarters, but I was in a private house. I was in Castlefinn for my headquarters. H. J. Kelly was (Battalion O/C) transport officer and a good fellow. His brother maybe was in charge of transport. Seán McCoole was Brigade Adjutant, a teacher. They weren't very active there and they didn't want to stay out and fight. We had Peadar O'Donnell

31   Jim Lane was the engineering officer for the Clonakilty Battalion, Cork No. 3 Brigade, in the War of Independence, and joined other Cork officers in Donegal during the Civil War.
32   Denis Galvin of Bandon (not to be confused with the North Cork IRA officer, Denis Galvin) operated a mechanics garage, and was active in the West Cork IRA. His son John served as a Fianna Fáil TD in Cork city.
33   James O'Sullivan commanded the Bantry (town) company, in the Bantry Battalion of the IRA. He was a telegraphist in Bantry Post Office.
34   Tom Mullins, not John as in the original text, was active in the Cork No. 3 Brigade, until his arrest in July 1920. Following his release from prison, he joined the Cork IRA contingent in Ulster. He later served as the chairman of the Fianna Fáil party, and was both a TD and a Senator.
35   Con Crowley was an active Volunteer from a prominent Republican family in Kilbrittain.

on the Div[isional] Staff and very sound he was. He was a TD there. Once we met Joe Sweeney at the start of the Civil War.[36] He came to meet us to give us pardon and to allow us to get out of Donegal with a free pass and safe conduct to Charlie Daly who was in charge, for Seán Lehane had gone to Dublin. Charlie Daly arranged a meeting. He took 4 or 5 of us into Churchtown and the meeting lasted for a few hours. Galvin and Con Crowley were there. Charlie and Sweeney were great friends and they had many things to talk over. Sweeney had 3 or 4 of his officers with him there. [Tom] Glennon, a Derry q[uarter]master who was a poisonous pill.[37] **[98R]** We refused to go out of the area. Ireland was all the same to us, and we were as happy to fight in Donegal as in Cork, but Joe Sweeney was upset.

Truce: We had a scrap with him in Newtownhamilton.[38] We were billeted in a little village when 7 or 8 lorries of Free State troops ran in on us and they opened fire. We returned the fire. We had been across the border the night before and on our return we had billeted there. The Free Staters had 9 or 10 casualties. Five of their lorries got through but they left 4 or 5

---

36   Civil War is written as C/W in the original text.
37   Tom Glennon had served in the Belfast IRA before becoming an officer in the National Army. He gained a bad reputation among Republicans during the Civil War.
38   Newtownhamilton is in County Armagh, not far from the border with the south. In *Donegal & the Civil War, The Untold Story* (Cork 2011), pp. 104–107, Liam Ó Duibhir reports that four National Army soldiers were killed and three wounded in the exchange on 4 May 1922.

motorcars and took to the field, and we got the motorcars. We took the rifles off those we had shot for there were a good few killed and wounded. Next day or so an armistice was signed. There was a row on in Kilkenny at the time, so they came up to Raphoe a few days later and they signed the peace terms.[39] There were none of our men wounded that day. Seán Lehane was in front of a door and the first shot struck just above his head. It was [Tom] Glennon from Derry who fired it, I'm sure. And Seán being in full uniform was conspicuous enough. We went across the border in strength. We had a few skirmishes at Lifford, across the bridge, not much, this was only a dozen shots or so, on 9 or 10 different days before this. There were about 70 of us who went in to attack a camp of their's inside the border. We went by lorry to the boundary nearly, and then we went in on foot. We went in a good piece to this camp. We opened fire on the camp but they returned the fire very quickly. Their **[98L]** spies on our side were able to tell them that we were coming. Even then in Donegal we used to be fired on when we were in billets. Special Constables operated in Donegal up to the Treaty (EOM: *and I suppose their complete organisation was left behind when the B Specials were no longer Specials*).[40] We took over a house of a commandant in the Specials. They put us in a back room but we wanted front rooms, and we threw

39   Fighting between pro- and anti-Treaty troops occurred in Kilkenny in the last week of April.
40   The Ulster Special Constabulary, comprising A, B and C Specials, was a reserve police force set up in Northern Ireland in October 1920.

out sentries. And next morning all of them were gone, he and the daughter and the family, and we had the house to ourselves. Their valuables were locked up in special room. 'I'll give you the key to go into this room whenever you like,' I said to the girl but she wouldn't go in. In Raphoe we were in a barracks and the Free Staters had another barracks, but there was no cooperation at all.

Civil War: We had left Raphoe and Drumboe was a few miles away. Charlie Daly decided to go west, and we went on to Glenveigh Castle, where we stayed a while. Charlie attacked and we captured a few Free State lorries and we captured the soldiers and arms across the county from Glenveigh. Next morning Seán Lehane arrived.**[99R]** Larkin was with us there.[41] He had been a Brigade O/C in the Second Northern Division. As we had a lot of unattached fellows with us Seán L[ehane] decided to form a column and then contact the enemy. The Free State troops were no damned good. They surrounded a billet at Castlefinn and withdrew again. Seamus Cotter who was in charge said they'd fight, but the Free State withdrew when our men would not surrender. [Joe] Sweeney wasn't looking for [a] fight (EOM: *I suppose the prestige of Daly and Lehane and the*

41   Seán Larkin, O/C of Tyrone No. 3 Brigade, was executed at Drumboe Castle in March 1923 with Charlie Daly, Dan Enright and Tim O'Sullivan. The four men were arrested at Meenabaul, Dunlewey (County Donegal), and sentenced to death in January 1923, but the sentence was suspended. However, two months later the men were executed as an unofficial reprisal for the death of a National Army officer.

others overwhelmed the Donegal Free Staters). We had only 100 armed men in Donegal and Sweeney must have had 1,000 men and the people. At first the people ignored us, but later they were getting to like us. The best crowd were the Presbyterians for they knew that we were fighting for a principle, and they said that the others fought for pay. 8 of us were surrounded in a house when we were in bed and the shot came through the window. The Free Staters had about 200 men. They kept it up for about 4 or 5 hours, but then they withdrew, and they left us where we were. This was in Ardara or somewhere near to it. Seven or 8 of us had gone away from the main column to locate good positions. Then, as the column was too big, we divided into 3 groups. The fellows used to be starved with the hunger for some people would give us nothing. There were a crowd of us, Mullins and Seán Lehane, and Con Crowley, Denis Galvin and I remained together. Charlie Daly was in charge of another crowd and he was coming to meet us **[99L]** with 4 or 5 others for they and we intended then to get out of Donegal. We waited for them but had we remained for another half hour we would have been captured. We had commandeered a boat and a crew to row us to Sligo shore at night. It was now after midnight and we thought we would never see the other side of Donegal Bay. Billy Pilkington, who was Div[isional] O/C there, met us and we went on to Argina where Bofin had a whole area where there was not a Free State soldier. There were a crowd of up to 100 there, and a fine lot of men they were.

Then we got city clothes and we handed all our arms to Bofin, which were to have been sent on, but I don't know if they ever were sent on.[42] Seán Lehane met Liam Lynch and Lynch gave him £5. He had no money. Kathleen McLoughlin and Roisin Doherty, Pa Murray's wife, was with us. God what they used to suffer in Donegal sometimes, for they'd be around with us for a week at a time. We were then sent by Lynch to take charge of the 2nd Eastern Division, Seán L[ehane], Mullins and I. The others went back to Cork. We were arrested by pure chance due to the generosity of the woman of the house. **[100R]** At 2 a.m. we had gone to bed but she hadn't much food in the house, so she went into the town … to buy butcher's meat, but he was too quick for her, for I suppose she wasn't accustomed to buy much of it, and he went to or sent on this information to the enemy so we were surrounded unarmed.[43] We were in Wexford for 3 or 4 nights, where they treated us badly. Seán and I were shifted in an armoured car to Dublin then, and it was a pal from Ballykinlar who shifted us.[44] We stopped on the way and he bought us a half pint of whiskey on the road up. We thought we were in for it and we were prepared, but we didn't care a damn. The night we were first sent to Kilmainham. We were

---

42 Paul Bofin, Republican flying column commander in the Sligo area during the Civil War.

43 Fitzgerald was arrested on 8 January 1923, at Ballyduff, Ferns, County Wexford, along with Seán Lehane, Martin Howlett, Phil Lennon and Patrick Fitzpatrick. *The Freeman's Journal*, 10 January 1923.

44 Armoured car is written as a/car in the original text, here and elsewhere.

kept 5 or 6 weeks and then left in with the rest of the prisoners. There were a good number of prisoners there. We were caught in December [1922] and we spent January and February there. There was a decent Free State officer in charge of the gaol.[45] He was mild and he would never say anything nasty to a prisoner. Then we were shifted to the Joy, where Paudeen O'Keeffe was the Deputy Governor, who knew both of us well …'[46] 'I'll never forget the good days I had in Kilbrittain,' he said, for he was a Sinn Féin organiser there.

'I hope you'll give us as good a time now,' I said to him.

He was a little pimp of a divileen, but fair play to him, he wasn't bad. He had a revolver strapped on each leg. The regulations were tightened up there. Seán Lehane was O/C of A Wing most of the time. I was in a cell with Con Leary from Kerry, a grand fellow, he was, and [100L] we pulled great together, the two of us.[47] Con had been sentenced to death in Kerry. He had never been reprieved, but the sentence was never carried out. Seán was told by someone inside and we could be executed alright. Paudeen and Seán would fight like 2 dogs: every day they were at it for they wouldn't let the world go with each other. He talked like a British Tommy, f— and blinding,

---

45   Officer is written as O² in the original text.
46   Patrick 'Paudeen' O'Keeffe (not O'Keefe as in the original text) was a Corkman closely associated with Michael Collins. He was a pro-Treaty TD, the deputy governor of Mountjoy Gaol during the Civil War, and later the secretary-general of the GAA.
47   Con Leary (or O'Leary) of the Kerry No. 2 Brigade helped lead the Republican defence of Kilmallock during July 1922.

and it was something shocking to listen to. Seán was a good type of an O/C. Cosgrave the governor was a real gentleman always.[48] There were always rows in gaol. They tried to make us recognise them directly, and not through our own officers. They tried to lock us up but we busted every door in the place. They locked us in the wing and then they stopped our parcels, letters, laundry. And in the morning we had to be fed one by one. Military orderlies came around with food but the prisoners busted door after door, and the armed sentry was shoved into a cell and their military orderlies were locked in also. Our lads put a book behind the doors and busted the hinges of the doors. And some of them took off the cell doors. A **[101R]** firing party came in then. The Free Staters ordered us to go back into our cells with a firing party. Then they ordered us to go out into the yard. I was on No. 2 landing and so was Seán Lehane. They brought in hoses and they flooded us and our cells. Then they dragged us out one by one and they left us outside in the open. They threw us about every way as they were trying to land us out and they left us outside for the night in our wet clothes. In the morning we came in for our breakfast. They had the doors repaired then, for they had worked all night on them, and we were brought into the wing 2 by 2, and we were locked up. An armoured car had been around us all night outside. For that day inside we

---

48   Philip Cosgrave, older brother of William T. Cosgrave, was active in the Irish Volunteers and a Sinn Féin TD for Dublin. He was governor of Mountjoy until his premature death in 1923.

were quiet. They had to open the door to feed us and then we broke them again. Then they left us alone. They shifted all the prisoners to the Curragh, but I wouldn't go. 'Would you like a shift?' they'd say and when I replied 'No', they'd leave you alone.

Hunger strike: Nearly every man in the wing went on it. I wasn't too gone about it for I had been 10 or 11 days in Cork Gaol once when I had been given 3 months for unlawful assembly in 1919. We wouldn't disperse when they wanted us to disperse, then the RIC fired over our heads as we came out the door, for they had gone into the barracks for their rifles. Whilst we were inside in Cork Gaol there had been a hunger strike.[49] And when we got what we had been fighting for we came off the strike. Mick Fitz[gerald] of N[orth] Cork was there at the time for the Fermoy disarming.[50] **[101L]** At Mountjoy I used to say, 'let us go on a strike but let us leave the camps alone', for others had got in touch with the camps. They tried to shift me several times but I was against it. I shifted from one wing to another so they could not catch me. Frank Barrett was O/C [of] the wing and I was O/C of a landing.[51] Each day Barrett would be

49   Hunger strike is written as h/strike in the original text.
50   Michael Fitzgerald, Irish Transport and General Workers' Union organiser and Cork No. 2 Brigade officer, was arrested for his part in the disarming of a British Army church party in Fermoy, during which one soldier was killed. Fitzgerald led the Cork Gaol hunger strike of August to November 1920, in which he, Joe Murphy and Terence MacSwiney (in Brixton) died.
51   The Republicans created a military structure for their prisons, with officers selected to command jail landings (a row of cells) and wings (a separated group of landings). Frank Barrett of Mid-Clare served on the IRA Executive.

in bed and he'd write out something that had to be read to each prisoner. This was the 20th day but I had never refused to take his written proclamations. Military came into the wing. 'Pack up you're going to …'

But I finished my hunger strike there. Barrett came off the strike on the 21st day. Malloney and others came off after 28 days.[52] Some fellows suffered a power. I had no pain or ache. I saw fellows in an awful state for they had to get injections to keep their bowels open. And others had fierce bad diarrhoea. I used to take a dose of salts every day. A doctor came in when we were 34 days, then a specialist came and he examined me and he said nothing except, 'There's no fear for him for a long time yet.' I collapsed the day I came off the strike. When the hunger strike **[102R]** started the Free Staters brought in food every day for 2 weeks or so and they left it inside the gate.[53] And for a while they would dish it out to us in our wing cell by cell. All in our wing were on strike, for if you came off the strike you were shifted at once, so no food then came in to tempt us nor did we see other fellows taking food. Seán Russell came along to tell us the strike was off.[54] I was released about a fortnight afterwards.

Wexford: Martin Howlett and Tom Howlett and Bob

---

52   It is not known who Malloney was.
53   Hunger strike is written as h/s in the original text.
54   Seán Russell was an IRA GHQ staff officer and later controversial chief of staff of the IRA during the Second World War.

Lambert who was in charge of a column there.[55] He was a fine fellow and the others were as fine a crowd as ever I met. Maybe they hadn't arms in the Tan War or their officers were bad, and that was the reason they didn't fight then. (Pilkington had captured every Free State post in Leitrim for that was Pilkington's boast. When we left Donegal our leaving released a pile of Free State soldiers there.) Charlie Daly told me that he had been at a Supreme Council (EOM: *of the IRB*) meeting by accident: and often he said to me, 'If I'm caught I'll pay for that meeting.' What kind of a meeting was it? The one that took the vote on the Treaty? Dick Barrett hadn't his boots on when he was shot, for that came out at the inquest on his body when it was delivered by the Fianna Fáil government.[56] The ordinary soldiers who were on the putting out of us in the Joy were only half hearted about it.

T[an] W[ar]: Fellows on the run inside: there was a lot of changing of names in Ballykinlar to conceal identity. We would parade in the **[102L]** camp in front of a hut for identification, but we could never see who was looking at us; or we would be led in front of an officer.

C[ivil] W[ar]: In Kilmainham a prisoner was put in with

55 South Wexford Brigade officers Martin Howlett (brigade intelligence officer), Tom Howlett (brigade O/C) and Robert Lambert (column commander).

56 Dick Barrett, former Cork No. 3 Brigade quartermaster and Four Courts staff officer, was executed with Rory O'Connor, Liam Mellows and Joe McKelvey in Mountjoy Gaol in December 1922 as a reprisal for the IRA assassination of Seán Hales, TD.

Seán Lehane and I, and he remained with us a week and then he disappeared again. He was a Dublin man but no one inside knew him. We suspected him from the beginning and he was a very talkative fellow about the war. 'I won't be inside a week, but I'll be out,' he said. He was always asking us where we were during the fighting, but we were careful.

Tadg [O']Sullivan in Skib[bereen] area was a great quartermaster.[57] Seán Lehane and I were in Bandon and we wanted to go to the pictures and Seán Hales who was brigade O/C also.[58] He asked Tadg for a few bob and Tadg gave him 5 shillings.

Deasy surrender:[59] We were to have met Liam Deasy in Kilkenny when we were in Wexford, for he sent word to us to come and meet him. Afterwards in Mountjoy he said he wanted us to discuss the position with him. Seán Lehane was taken to see Liam Deasy in Portobello. Liam then told Seán what he was doing. Then Seán came back and he told me what Deasy was doing. I said, 'why didn't he die as well as the rest?',

---

57   Tadg O'Sullivan served as the Cork No. 3 Brigade quartermaster during the War of Independence and Civil War, in charge of arms and supplies. He was a brother of GHQ adjutant-general Gearóid O'Sullivan.

58   Fitzgerald seems to have confused Seán Hales with his brother Tom. Seán served as a battalion commander (in charge of the 1st Battalion, Cork No. 3 Brigade), while Tom Hales acted as brigade commander (in charge of the Cork No. 3 Brigade in 1919–20 and again in 1922–23.)

59   In January 1923 National Army troops arrested Liam Deasy in Kilkenny and sentenced him to death. He then issued a public appeal to his IRA colleagues for an 'immediate and unconditional surrender of all arms and men'.

but Seán said, 'dead men are no use to us now.' **[103L]** Liam Deasy had heard or had seen the Free State dig a grave for him inside.

'As a senior officer inside I am taking responsibility,' said Seán Lehane.

Burning of Loyalist houses [1921]: In Inishannon and in Bandon. Sealy King, who was a D.J. [District Justice] a magistrate, was taken prisoner and Lord Bandon was also taken but escaped.[60] The British were very worried about him. General Peacocke in Inishannon's house [*sic*] was burned.[61] We used to burn 3 houses for the one they burned of ours.

Father Devine, a Jesuit, gave a retreat in 1923 in either May or June. He raised a cross on high and he called the cross of Christ down on Republicans and upon their supporters in the town. This priest used to go into the barracks and beat the prisoners there. Jeff... O'Connor, a priest, shot some of the lads and he is now in the Department of Defence.

Sergeant Hogan of Kilbrittain [RIC].

60 The IRA took hostage four loyalist magistrates in June 1921 – Charles Sealy King, John St Leger Gillman, John James Fitzpatrick and the Earl of Bandon – to prevent the possible execution of Republican prisoners. King escaped his captors. The Earl of Bandon was released during the Truce.

61 Lt Colonel Warren Peacocke, a retired military officer and suspected informer in West Cork, was shot dead by the IRA in 1921.

Maurice 'Mossy' Donegan

(UCDA P17b/108, pp. 73–84)[1]

 Maurice 'Mossy' Donegan (1899–1904) was a native of Bantry who served in senior command positions with the IRA in West Cork and Ulster, and fought on the Republican side during the Civil War. A noted Gaelic footballer, he represented Cork at county level. In 1924 Donegan graduated from University College Cork and became a national schoolteacher. He was principal of the Model School in Cork, retiring in 1968. His lifelong interest in farming led to a close association with, and ultimately chairmanship of, the Cork Co-Operative Marts. During the Second World War Donegan served in the National Army with the rank of major, in command of the 31st Battalion. He settled in Bandon with his wife and family. He remained active in Old IRA fraternal associations until his death in 1974.

***

[73R] I went North with Fitz.[2] Our 20 to 40 men were to have

---

1 Maurice 'Mossy' Donegan also made a statement to the BMH – WS 639.
2 Jack Fitzgerald – see previous interview. It is not clear when this took place.

had nuisance value and could be used to produce a political or diplomatic effect. There were questions asked about them (EOM: *or were expected to be asked*) in the Northern Parliament.[3] British troops crossed the border at Belleek [Fermanagh] and at Pettigo [Donegal] after our lads had sniped them. Provisional Government troops came up of their own accord and then the Br[itish] withdrew.[4] We had 2 or 3 Lewis guns. Where did we get them?

In May we went to the North. We went by lorry to Dublin where we were briefed in McKelvey's office in the Four Courts.[5] We were to draw the anger of the British, be backed up by the Free State (EOM: *he means Provisional Govt troops*) and then we would all get drawn in to the fight. Raphoe [Donegal] was our headquarters. There was a clash at Newtown Cunningham [Donegal] [with the National Army]. The fellows in the F[our] C[ourts] were quite happy about this and serious. This clash finished what we set out to do for it finished any hope of our relationship with the Provisional Government improving, for they were getting worse. When we looked for help from the Free State it was refused.

3   Parliament is written as Parlt in the original text.
4   Provisional Government is sometimes shortened to Prov Govt and sometimes P/G in the original text.
5   Joe McKelvey, not McElvey as in the original text, was an IRA leader from Belfast who briefly became the anti-Treaty IRA's chief of staff in late June 1922 before being captured during the fall of the Four Courts. A member of the IRA Executive, he was one of four leaders executed in December 1922 as a reprisal for the assassination of Seán Hales, TD.

A few houses were burned to see would any reprisals be taken on the Donegal side of the border.

Drumboe Castle [Donegal]: When we were east of Raphoe we got word that they (EOM: *the 6 county government*) were on the border and we sent out word to the Free State in Drumboe and we said we were going on to the border, but their dispatch rider **[73L]** said they were keeping in touch with events and if they (EOM: *6 counties*) crossed they'd operate. I don't think they had crossed at the time.

I was in charge of our crowd. We would patrol mostly at night from 30 to 40 men, or maybe from 20 to 30, for I was Brigade O/C of the Raphoe area, and Jack Fitzgerald from Kilbrittain South had another brigade. Really we had brigade areas for we had not got brigades. (EOM: *the majority of the men had gone over to the Provisional Government?*)

In one village, was it Clady, I saw 'To Hell with the Pope' and 'Hell Roast the Pope'. I gave them a week to take down the notices, or rather to wipe them out. I stood on a barrel and addressed them. Everyone in the village. All the men were first assembled and I gave them orders about taking down or clearing away such notices. We were helped with guns from Beggar's Bush[6] and a consignment had been sent from Cork to B[eggar's] B[ush] to replace them.[7]

---

6   Beggar's Bush Barracks in Dublin was taken over from the British Army by the IRA in January 1922 and it became the military headquarters for the National Army.

7   In an arrangement brokered between Michael Collins and Liam

[74R] A few days before the C[ivil] W[ar] I came from the mountain in Donegal and I had a long ... so with Lehane and Harry Boland I went south.[8] In a few days time there was an attack on Skibbereen and I was ordered to remain in the south and go on to Skib[bereen]. Lehane and I went to Baltimore to go to the North by sea. We got a fishing smack and a captain, but he refused to go beyond Mizen Head with us, for there was a big sea running.[9] A barrel of oil which was not lashed was aboard, and I spent my whole time dodging it as it was slashed around by the seas. We came back that night and we went on to Skib[bereen] that next morning for the attack, and I was ordered by Deasy to stay in Skib[bereen].

One gun which we had came from Kerry; another gun, a big one, Moylan owned but I'm not sure of that now.[10] We

Lynch during May 1922, anti-Treaty IRA forces exchanged rifles with the National Army, whose weapons had been supplied by the British government. The anti-Treaty rifles were then used to arm the IRA operating in Northern Ireland. In this way, Collins attempted to hide his complicity in the IRA's Northern Ireland offensive.

8   Seán Lehane, a senior figure in the Cork No. 3 Brigade, commanded the Schull area and flying columns in 1920 and 1921. Lehane succeeded Liam Deasy as brigade commander during the Truce period, but resigned his position when Tom Hales was released from prison. In the Civil War, Lehane commanded Republican forces in Ulster during the border offensive.

9   Mizen Head, not Mizzen as in the original text, is a peninsula in County Cork.

10   Seán Moylan was leader of the Newmarket Battalion and later O/C of Cork No. 2 Brigade during the War of Independence, and fought on the Republican side in the Civil War. His forces did briefly own an ancient black powder cannon, but it blew up during a test firing, which Moylan described in BMH WS 505.

plonked one gun up at the windmill up over the RIC barracks in a row of small houses, and we put it resting on a platform of sandbags, and of course it was aimed as you'd aim a shotgun. There was a black powder charge and a conical ball of iron. There was a row of houses between us and the barracks for we were on the high ground. 100 yards away was another row of small houses and another 100 yards away was the barracks, which stood up above these houses. There was a touch hole but there was no one brave enough to stand beside the fuse, so we got out of the house and the fuse was lighted and off it went. Every one of us was watching the barracks, but there was a complete lack [74L] of any artillery information amongst us for we had pointed our artillery as you would point a stick. Everyone watched the barracks, then someone spotted a hole in the intervening house, a big hole it was, but in the roof. We shifted our cannon a bit then. The other gun was in the bank, 100 yards from the RIC barracks, and the gun was on the same level as one of the top rooms of the bank. I wasn't there but I know what happened to this gun. The gun was set then our fellows left the room. Then there was a fearsome explosion. 'Where's our gun?' said one of the lads, looking through the smoke.

'That's not the point,' said the bank manager, 'but where's the bank?'

There was no one hurt on our side. The room was destroyed.

We brought down the other gun to a house next to the

barracks and there was only a lane way between them. We tore a hole in our wall and we pointed out the gun and we decided to have another go. And didn't it blow a hole both through the outside wall of the barracks **[75R]** facing in and through the inside wall of the dividing wall of the barracks and the projectile dropped inside in a floor where some of the Free State lads were having a chat. Jer McCarthy was there.[11] He was a good individual soldier but a bit of a lunatic, and I'm [sure] that's what made them surrender, for they surrendered soon after that. The big gun was mounted on two wheels, but it was a devil to shift it.

The small one was in the bank and that was the one that blew up. The big one was very impressive, especially to the people who were firing it. A fellow was shot through the stomach over it, for there was so much damn trouble connected with it at the beginning when it was being shifted into the small houses.

Lehane and I came down from Donegal for a meeting. We filled in a Crossley tender with mines in the Four Courts, intending to bring it up to the North. This was a tender which I had brought up with me from Bandon; a British Crossley it was, which we commandeered from Kelly in Bantry.[12] We filled it up with mines in the Courts. I was told later that it was struck by a shell during the attack on the Four Courts. We were due to return to Donegal and I was in the Clarence [Hotel]

11   Jeremiah McCarthy, not MacCarthy as in the original text, was an active officer from Schull.
12   It is not known who Kelly is.

where I was in bed with Seán MacSwiney and Liam Deasy.[13] I heard the sound of [75L] guns, and then I knew that the attack had started. The sound woke me up. We went down to the billiard room, and we were hardly in when a group of men rushed in with rifles and a fellow who I knew from Ballykinlar was in there first.[14] They had come in by the back. There were a small crowd of them there and we were going to pull guns when I recognised this fellow. Lehane and I go on to Harcourt Street to No. 6. The Countess [Markievicz] was there filling a revolver, which was broken open on her lap.[15] I don't know what happened when Boland, Lehane, and I decided to go or why, or I don't know where we got the car from, but we drove on out [of Dublin].[16] We were stopped about 50 times, but we got through. We stayed in Tipp[erary] in a place which Harry Boland knew, a farmhouse, and we came as far as Clonmel, for we were in the barracks, but I don't know who was there. We went on to Mallow, Lehane and I, but Boland stayed in … Culhane and Hyde were there in Mallow also.[17] Deasy and

13   Seán MacSwiney was Cork No. 1 Brigade's quartermaster and brother of Terence.
14   Donegan is talking here about the time he spent in Ballykinlar Internment Camp in County Down, during the War of Independence.
15   Sinn Féin maintained its Dublin headquarters at 6 Harcourt Street in Dublin. The IRA commonly used the British Webley service revolver, which snapped open at its centre to allow access to load the ammunition chambers.
16   Donegan is referring to the subsequent dispute that arose over whether or not the Cork officers had promised to abstain from the fighting when National Army officers allowed them to depart.
17   These men were both staff officers in the IRA's 1st Southern Division. Seán Culhane of Cork city was the divisional intelligence officer, while

Lynch were away, so **[76R]** Lehane and I decided that we
had no hope of getting up North by land. Lehane and I went
on to Skib[bereen] and it was there that Deasy met us and
told us about the general situation. I think we must have been
in Skib[bereen] the night before the attack, for I remember
meeting a fellow who was going in to the barracks to fight
against us, and I walked as far as the barracks gate with him.

I was then sent on a column to Limerick, a column
from Cork 5 [Brigade] with about from 50 to 80 men. Pete
Kearney was there in Tipp.[18] I went up as far as the outskirts
of Limerick city, and there we were told to hold a line around
Bruree and Kilmallock. Sandow was in the city [Limerick],
with the remnants of fellows from the city [Cork] and the
Kerry column.[19] Con Leary was in charge of Limerick, and I
was second in charge.[20] The others went through us when we
retired and we were the last to leave Limerick.

We remained in Bruree and Kilmallock until Bruree was
attacked one morning.[21] The garrison put up a poor fight and

Seán Hyde served as a senior staff officer. The Division headquarters was
in Mallow.
18 Pete Kearney was O/C of the Dunmanway Battalion in Cork No. 3 Brigade.
19 Dan 'Sandow' O'Donovan, a highly active IRA officer from Cork city, was
vice-commander of Cork No. 1 Brigade at the outbreak of the Civil War.
20 Con Leary (or O'Leary), a national teacher from Killarney, was active in
the Rathmore area and served as Kerry No. 2 Brigade quartermaster. He
directed IRA operations during the extended fighting in the Kilmallock
area in July and early August 1922.
21 Sustained combat occurred between the IRA and the National Army in
the Bruff-Bruree-Kilmallock area in the last two weeks of July 1922. The
Bruree attack occurred on 28 July 1922.

then surrendered. I was in Ash Hill Towers in Kilmallock, which was our headquarters. We had I think a Cork city column, a Kerry or 2 Kerry columns, a Limerick col[umn], and a West Cork col[umn], up to 300 men. We counter-attacked, and Childers was there this morning.[22] This was the first time I had met him. He came along the line with me for he was then **[76L]** a reporter, because he wrote an account of that action, and I remember a phrase, 'watching and guarding their beloved Republic'. Next morning I went in a bloody big armoured car which had been made in Cork. It was made of iron, not steel, and was called 'The River Lee'. It had been put [on] the body of a lorry; four pieces of iron an inch thick. There was no ventilation grill and it was so hot inside that you wanted to strip off your clothes. We captured most of the town back again, save a bit, and then there came along a solid-tyred (EOM: *Free State*) [armoured car], a big one, which opened up on us with its Vickers [machine-gun]. One of their bullets came into the car and it buzzed along on the inside. We used to stick out our guns through the holes and fire. This was at the attack on Brown's house – the Minister's – I saw Childers walking around the road in quite a dangerous place, but he didn't seem to take any cover, whether it was that he had the situation summed up or not, I don't know. **[77R]** To me there seemed no bloody sense to the way he was moving about. He

22   Erskine Childers was a noted author and Republican propagandist, who was executed by the Free State government on 24 November 1922.

just marched around there. 'The River Lee' was very heavy and it could only move on main roads (EOM: *and there were not many main roads then in being*). In the evening I went back to Ash Hill Towers. About this time the Staters landed below in Passage [near Cork city], and the Cork 1 column was called back at once. The Free Staters landed in Fenit and the Kerry column went back.[23] Our line was thinned then and the Free Staters brought in artillery. I saw the first shells as they dropped on the outskirts. Con Leary then went away. The artillery had a demoralising effect on our troops when it hit some of the buildings. I met a half column going back, and I had to put them ahead of me again. Deasy then rang me up and I reported to him about our situation and about the men who had tried to run away. 'They'll be in here without any delay,' he said. 'For so and so held them until we got out of Buttevant.' They had us surrounded by then.

We retired to Charleville, held it. We were reinforced by Seán Hyde who had a troop of cavalry, from 30 to 40 horses.[24] The Free Staters had high ground to the south-west in front, and I suggested to Hyde to charge this hill. He had been having an awful damn time to get oats for the horses. After a survey we found barbed [77L] wire around the bottom of the hill, and a huge wide deep drain filled with water. We withdrew.

23   The National Army landed at Fenit on 2 August and Passage West on 8 August 1922.

24   An IRA cavalry unit operated from Ballincollig Barracks in the early stages of the Civil War, commanded by Seán Hyde, a veterinary student.

The Free Staters had landed in Courtmacsherry south of Bandon, between 200 to 300 of them.[25] We got on a train, was it n[orth] of Mallow? We examined Mallow Bridge, but we got over it and got back to Cork. The Free State were quite close to Cork when we got in. Evacuation was on next morning of the city so we went on to West Cork.[26] We formed a column in West Cork. Cork 3 [Brigade] stayed here and we went west. Dan Holland was here at the time.[27]

Barry and I attacked Ballineen with 2 columns. It is a village along the road on which Free State posts were spread out and they had an armoured car. We captured a fair show of stuff and some of their positions, but we lost 3 or 4 men.[28] We took our prisoners with us.

We attacked Bantry and captured ¾ of it. We got rifles and ammunition, and we lost 4 men.[29] Ted [O']Sullivan, Gibbs Ross, [78R] and I were there.[30] At that stage we could do what we liked, for we held the towns.

25 The landing actually took place at Union Hall, near Skibbereen on 8 August. Courtmacsherry was not occupied until the second week of September.
26 Republicans evacuated Cork city on 10 August 1922.
27 Dan Holland was an active and senior IRA officer in West Cork.
28 The attack on the adjoining villages of Ballineen and Enniskeane took place on 4 November 1922. John Howell (Clonakilty) and Tadhg O'Leary (Macroom) were killed.
29 The attack on 30 August cost the lives of Commandant Gibbs Ross (Bantry), Captain Patrick Cooney (Skibbereen), Lt Donal McCarthy (Ballydehob) and Lt Michael Crowley (Glandore). In the original text rifles and ammunition is written as R[1] and amm.
30 Gibbs Ross was O/C of the Cork No. 5 Brigade. For Ted O'Sullivan, see his interview.

I was mostly in Kerry. I met 'Free' Murphy and John Joe Rice.[31]

Fr Duggan came out one day when Barry was there. I always carried a gun when I heard of that. Ted [O']Sullivan went there but Barry's wife came out with Fr Duggan.[32] The people were fed up with the whole thing. The bridges were down, roads were impassable, the railways were gone and they couldn't see any end to this thing. As well, there was the danger of getting shot. Our friendly people were eaten out of house and home. Their horses and cattle had been taken away.

There was only one of our men of any prominence in Bantry who went Free State. In 1919, when I was Brigade O/C he was battalion V/C.[33]

Ted [O']Sullivan sent out word to me from Cork gaol, 'whatever you do, don't be captured'. There was another chap with me and the Free State had the place surrounded, and two Free Staters called into me in the village. John Mullins was with me on my right side when these two called over. Connolly put in the gun to his belly.[34] 'Put them up John,' he said, for he knew him. Mullins had a Peter [the Painter].[35] Behind the

31 Humphrey 'Free' Murphy was O/C of the Kerry No. 1 Brigade in the Civil War; John Joe Rice was O/C of the Kerry No. 2 Brigade in 1922.

32 Leslie Price married Tom Barry during the Truce period. A veteran of the Easter Rising, she served as a senior organiser for Cumann na mBan in Cork.

33 This was Tom Ward.

34 No information could be found on Mullins or Connolly.

35 The semi-automatic broom-handled Mauser .96 pistol was popularly known as a 'Peter the Painter'. During the 1911 'Siege of Sydney Street' in London, anarchist gunman Peter 'the Painter' Piaktow used the pistol to hold off police, hence its nickname.

two Free Staters, 5 or 6 other Free Staters were **[78L]** coming down. I had a rifle stuck into my belly. I got out my short Webley [revolver] and as I knew that the man with the rifle would be faster, I shot him first. I could see Mullins' hands moving, as if to draw his Peter, before he put his hands up. I got the two of them. The fellows behind us opened fire but we threw ourselves down and we rolled back around the corner. There was a civilian shot dead and 2 or 3 were wounded.

In December 1924 I was allowed back home by the Free Staters.

Jack Lane could tell you what any sound was at night, whether it was a fox or one man or two men. He had a glass eye. With the least effort he always got out of trouble in the Tan War. He was in Ted [O']Sullivan's column and he was a … around Midleton.[36]

The county fellows who believed in freedom for its own sake were upset at the politics – [the] military crowd in Dublin who had let us down. It was well these men could not **[79R]** discuss documents, but they knew what freedom was.[37]

T[an] W[ar]: Four of us who had been at communion and were dressed up to kill, ran into a round-up early on outside of Bantry. The Liverpool Regiment, a decent crowd, and for that we might as well thank the colonel in charge, opened fire

---

36 Midleton, not Middleton as in the original text.
37 Apparently a reference to Éamon de Valera's 'Document Number 2', which he offered as a potential alternative to the Anglo-Irish Treaty.

on us, but we had nothing on us. The police with them didn't recognise us. They put us in a galvanised shed in front of the guard room, and at half 12 at night [the] RIC came up yelling for our blood, but the sergeant turned out the guard. The RIC had come right up to where we were but the sergeant and the guard drove them out. This was on the 20th of November 1920. We were there for a few days in Bantry when we were shifted by cruiser. Four of us [were] specially picked and sent by sea to Cobh. There we were transferred to a boat, in charge of which were the Essex Regiment. They didn't touch me but Barney [O']Driscoll, now in Portroe, C[ounty] Tipp[erary], who was elderly had grown a beard and they hopped off and hammered him.[38] Me they threatened, but they didn't beat me.

We were interviewed in the Detention Barracks in Cork. I was teaching in Carrick-on-Suir from January 1920 to April 1920, and before that we had raided the mail boat in Bantry. We had taken from 6 to 8 rifles and 6 revolvers, a lot of amm[unition], [79L] Verey Light [flare] pistols.[39] I was in charge of the raid. We captured a guard of sailors in a ship which was in at the quay. We had it well-timed. We held up the guard on deck, battered them down, 12 or 12 [sic] of them, and threatened them not to make any noise. I only saw 1 armed man, but their rifles were near them. There was a 3 inch gun mounted on the bow but we didn't think of the gun then, for

---

38   See Barney O'Driscoll's testimony earlier in this book.
39   The ship seizure at Bantry pier took place on 17 November 1919.

this was about the end of 1919. At that time we were making pikes. I remember putting a pike head into a pike in Seán Lehane's house.

We were in Cork prison for a few weeks and then we were put on board a destroyer. The weather was very bad and we were put down below where conditions were shocking. Seán Nolan, a TD who is now dead.[40] He was consumptive as I now realise, and when I looked at his face it was green and that must have made me sick, for I was sick until we reached Belfast. We had already heard of the [80R] gauntlet that prisoners had to run in Belfast. The fellow in charge of the escort said to us: 'You'll find that your people are worse friends of yours up there than we are.' A fellow was hit with a bar and he was taken to hospital, and a few of us got cracks from nuts and bolts. We were taken straight away to No. 1 Ballykinlar. We had to walk handcuffed from the train and carry our bags, and I know that the fellow I was handcuffed to was very small, and so he wasn't a good fit for me and it made it harder to walk.

Joe McGrath, the commandant, was released just after the Truce.[41] He made a tunnel from my hut. I was in charge of this, and it was a topping job. We could only go down 5 foot

40   Seán Nolan was elected to the Second Dáil in 1921, representing the Cork Mid, North, South, South-East and West constituency. He opposed the Anglo-Irish Treaty and was defeated in the 1922 General Election.

41   Joe McGrath, not MacGrath as in the original text, was director of intelligence in the National Army and intelligence chief of the CID. He also served as a TD from 1918 to 1924 and later founded the Irish Hospitals' Sweepstake.

… for then you struck the sea (EOM: *the camp is on a strand*). The ground was all sand. There was a cubicle in the end in which a latrine bucket was kept and we made a trap door in the wooden floor and we dug down. Right outside us was the wire and outside this again was the military road, which had to be propped up 6 feet from beneath, and then a fence 120 yards away, and it was behind this fence that we hoped we would rise up the end of our tunnel.

The sentry in No. 2 hut was right over us on a high platform. I said we must get some men who had experience of mining, so I sent over for [80L] John Hodnet[t], an old fellow who had been out in some bloody place in the USA. He was a Rosscarbery man but he had spent his life in the mines. I brought him over and he looked at what we were doing. 'You'll kill yourselves,' he said, 'for you can't prop it.' But we'd do anything short of suicide then to get out of this damned camp. We made frames, square frames and another three feet further on and outside of these frames we had bed boards which we cut in two. The legs of tables helped us for frames. There were bed boards on 3 sides, and with them we held up 3 ton lorries with only two feet of sand over the frames. We knew that in the First World War the German prisoners in England had got rid of every ounce of stuff they took out of the tunnel, but here we could stick the sand under our hut and spread it around on the sand inside in the camp. The hut was raised [81R] some distance from off the ground. The buckets were covered with papers.

We made a little railway of bed boards by cutting them in strips, and a trolley is now in Tadg Lynch's of Kenmare, the greatest man in Ireland to dig a tunnel – a draper. A man, we were told, wouldn't live when a candle would go out, but he lived for hours and worked when the candle went out through lack of air. We went astray in the making, for the tunnel became curved. Then I said, 'We'll put a bit of stick up, and sight on it.' Someone put up the stick, but I couldn't see a sight of it, but after a while someone said, 'Look where it is: it's up several feet', and here we were, back again right next to the sentry. We had used two men only at a time: one to work at the face and one to pull back the sand and we'd worked even when the military were around the hut, but we did not work at night.[42]

We boxed our compass better this time, and we went on straighter and we had candles then, for we could buy candles in the canteen and by sighting on them we could tell if we were going straight. We were within 2 or 3 yards of the fence when a company of engineers came into the 'Death Walk', which lay between 2 rows of barbed wire, and began to dig a trench. There were a couple of hundred men on the job and they struck the tunnel and they came into the hut through the tunnel. Three hundred **[81L]** bloody bed boards were gone, and that must have infuriated the camp staff as it showed up their laxity. I was Camp Commandant and in came the escort for me, and the

42   Jack Fitzgerald describes construction of the same tunnel in his testimony (see pp. 78–80).

Br[itish] officers were raging. They marched me off and the 25 men in the hut to [the] clink. We were court-martialled. There were two charges against me. I was Camp Commandant and I didn't report the digging of the tunnel; and (2) as it was in my hut I must have been working in it.

We had been at the tunnel for several weeks and we found it was no bother at all. We had a cookhouse of our own so we had meat skewers, choppers and shovels. The Tommies gave evidence of the finding of the tunnel. I was asked if I had anything to say. 'We are prepared to take anything that's coming,' I said, 'provided that any soldier here can swear that any of us were in the tunnel. Every man in this hut, or in the camp for that matter, could easily have had access to this tunnel.' Next day, the colonel said to me: 'For the sake of peace [we] will send you back to the camp.'

[82R] In the camp all the tables were crooked for there were legs missing from them.

The morale was good in Ballykinlar. When we first arrived in the camp the huts were coloured red but there was one small black hut in the middle, for scabies. There was a Colonel Little in charge, who belonged to the Black Watch, one of the regiments that guarded us; and he said to me, 'It's inconvenient for you not having an office to work in as Camp Commandant, and I was thinking of giving you a hut.' So he gave us this black hut, and we held our Camp Councils there. Dr O'Higgins, Seán Tracey of Kilkenny, Bernie [O']Driscoll, Tom Meldon of Dublin, Dr Dick Hayes and myself.[43] We were the Camp Council and there we discussed everything. This day we talked about helping the lads outside and the only way we could think of helping them was by holding as many troops as possible to guard us and for this reason we talked about burning the camp. Colonel Little used to come in on inspection. This day he came over. There was a sergeant major there also, who came over to me and said, 'What do you think would happen if there was a hut burned down in this camp?' Little said, 'We'll take bloody good care that more than that will happen,' as he turned on his heel and left me. [O']Higgins came over to me later when I told him. 'Oh God,' he said, 'a Dictaphone'. Then he pulled down the 3-ply boarding inside the hut and we found a Dictaphone.

[82L] Escape in Nov[ember]–Oct[ober] [1921]: there were 1,000 men in my camp at the Truce. We got in an old khaki suit in a parcel and parcels, if they were wrapped up in a certain coloured paper, would be left with the other parcels. We had a lad who could get in under this hut where the parcels were kept, pull back a board and get up into the hut. He would search for the parcels of a particular colour and remove them before they were censored. The uniforms had no buttons, but we pinned them up

---

43   Dr Thomas Francis O'Higgins was a Sinn Féin official in Portlaoise, and the brother of Kevin O'Higgins; for Bernie O'Driscoll, see his interview; Tom Meldon fought in the Easter Rising and acted as a musketry instructor for the Dublin Brigade during the War of Independence; Dr Richard Hayes was elected to the First Dáil and was a prominent supporter of the Anglo-Irish Treaty. No information could be found on Seán Tracey; however, prominent Kilkenny Republican Thomas Treacy was in Ballykinlar.

as best we could. At lock-up an escort came in and we lay under the hut near the gate. Paddy Colgan of Kildare, who joined the Free State and became a major and who lives in Killarney where he has a hotel, was with me.[44] During count there was a stuffed man in my bed and count was held about 9 o'clock. We had from 9 p.m. until the morning to get away …

After a while we marched out the gate. There was a PA and a sentry overhead in the cage.[45] As we passed the next sentry at the camp gate, an officer appeared and I advanced first and I saluted [and] so did Colgan. We went with the Tommies and **[83R]** crossed by ferry to Dundrum Bay in a boat. We had no buttons and no badges. We had trousers, coats and caps. A peculiar thing happened then. Our communications went out through a Sergeant Farrell, a Cavan man who was in the Br[itish] Army. We gave him a pound a week and more. I said, 'That bloody fellow, I don't trust him. Let's lay a trap for him.' But [Joe] McGrath said, 'The Cavan fellows say it's alright to trust him.' He had a special inside pocket made for dispatches. But he was nearly always tight, which was both suspicious and dangerous for us. Who did we see in civies but your man Farrell, when we got off the boat. He stopped and jumped back. Savage

44 See Patrick Colgan's account of the escape in BMH WS 850, Military Archives, Dublin. Paddy Colgan fought in the Easter Rising with the Maynooth Volunteers and later organised and commanded the North Kildare Battalion.

45 A PA (Póilíní Airm) is a military policeman.

had a call house in Dundalk.[46] 'We crawled out under the wire', I said, when he asked us how we got out, for I didn't trust him. He told us where Savage's was and he gave us a car. We drove off down to Newry, changed our clothes inside a house there, and off we headed for Dublin. Just north of Gormanstown Camp we found that there was a lorry drawn across the road. Both military and police were there, waiting for us. And an old RIC sergeant brought us back to Ballykinlar. Every road north and south was blocked and they were waiting for us at Ballykinlar Camp.

We were brought first to Drogheda Barracks. Their camp Intelligence Officer was a Captain Farran and when the tunnel was found he was in high glee. I said to him once, 'I'll get out of this place.' We were kept in an open lorry and four sentries were [83L] guarding us. At nightfall an officer came up to us. He was an Intelligence Officer, Captain Mathiesson. He had been in Ballykinlar before Farran. He was a Scots officer. 'Oh, here you are,' he said. 'Tough luck, would you like a drink?'

'It wouldn't do us any harm,' I said and he took us up to the canteen, where he gave us a drink. Next day in the guardroom your man Farran came down raging and he walked over to us.

'Fitzpatrick' was my name. In an ambush an RIC man saw me quite plainly at Aghagoheen and so I had to adopt a false name.[47] The RIC man had been badly wounded.[48] I stood up as

46 Possibly Bob Savage, an IRA activist from Newry.
47 Aghagoheen, not Agoheen as in the original text.
48 On 21 June 1920, Mossy Donegan, Seán Lehane and four others ambushed an RIC bicycle patrol on the Bantry to Durrus road. Constable

Farran pushed me back. He didn't know how I got out. Then over walks Capt[ain] Mathiesson whilst this was going on: 'Cheerio Fitzpatrick,' he said, 'I hope I'll see you under better circumstances.'

I was taken back to a field general court martial and was given six months hard labour and we were sent to Belfast Gaol. That was easily the cleanest prison I had been in. It was disciplined and we had to tow the line a bit ourselves.

[84R] The first morning we were in the yard we came down when it was dark, and I saw a group under an old roof and in front was Peadar Cronin who had a fair head.[49] John Fox, a sentenced prisoner, was there, and he was still under sentence of death.[50] He could get what he liked then, a bottle of beer a day and every day he brought me a bottle. I was in Belfast until the end of January [1922].

I went home straight. I wanted to get in touch. A fellow in Bantry, who in the early days was IRB, wanted to explain the advantages of the Treaty, but I think I hunted him out.

There was an order from the Division. They sent down for so many officers from the Brigade. When Tom Hales came out from gaol, Seán Lehane, who had been in charge of the brigade, resigned and handed it over to him.

Sullivan, an I[ntelligence] O[fficer]. Billy [O']Sullivan

James Brett was killed, while Sergeant Driscoll and another constable were wounded.

49   No information could be found about Peadar Cronin.

50   John Fox was a veteran Republican from Derry city.

an old Br[itish] soldier from Bantry, Dinny [O']Leary from Bantry,[51] now in Dublin, went North.

From the Four Courts we went on our first trip to the North. It was a kind of reconnaissance. Peadar O'Donnell was with us, and his brother Frank later came also. It was out of goodness they joined us.

Liam Lynch, Joe McKelvey, Rory O'Connor, Liam Mellows, we met in the Four Courts. Our people were very genuine there, for they accepted this attack on the North as a *via media* and one which would solve our problems.[52]

[84L] Joe O'Reilly was a *maidireen lahee* to Michael Collins.[53] I met him at a match in Dublin. 'I have a job,' said Joe O'Reilly, 'and I going to look after it.'

Dick McKee was doing engineering for us in the camp in Glandore, and he was absolutely sincere.[54] I was then at the Irish College in Ballingeary learning Irish, and I went over from there to Glandore. McKee inspired wonderful confidence. After that camp Cork was divided into brigades, for up to then it had been one brigade area. The men for that camp came from West Cork, and the camp had a good effect. McKee's presence and personality left a big impression on me.

51 Denis O'Leary. See Billy O'Sullivan's interview.
52 *Via media* is a Latin phrase that translates to 'the middle way'.
53 *Maidireen lahee* is a little dog in the mud. Joe O'Reilly was a close aide of Michael Collins.
54 This was the training camp organised by GHQ and held in August 1919. Dick McKee was commander of the IRA's Dublin Brigade. He was killed in British custody on 'Bloody Sunday', 21 November 1920.

TED O'SULLIVAN

(UCDA P17b/108, pp. 1–27)[1]

Ted O'Sullivan (1899–1971) was one of the top leaders of the IRA in West Cork. A native of Bantry, he participated in numerous IRA actions in 1920 and 1921. In August 1920 he was promoted to V/C of the Cork No. 3 Brigade, and filled the same position in the Cork No. 5 Brigade after its establishment. Taking the Republican side in the Civil War, he succeeded

Courtesy of Ted O'Sullivan, Cork (grandson)

Gibbs Ross as Brigade O/C in 1922. He was arrested during the Civil War and survived severe torture. Following his release from prison, O'Sullivan devoted himself to parliamentary politics, becoming a founding member and influential leader of Fianna Fáil. Elected to Dáil Éireann in 1937, he represented the Schull constituency until 1954. He also served as a senator from 1964 to 1969, and was a long-standing member of Cork County Council. Ted O'Sullivan died in 1971, in Cork city.

---

1   Although O'Malley had Tadg O'Sullivan at the top of his notes, Ted is the more common name by which O'Sullivan was known and has been used here to avoid any confusion. O'Sullivan also made a statement to the BMH, WS 1478, which he signed Ted.

THE MEN WILL TALK TO ME

[1R] The AOH were not strong in West Cork, for Bantry and Beara were strongholds of William O'Brien, and there the Redmondites had no hold.[2] The O'Brien people who came in first, then it was forgotten. About March of 1920 I was Brigade V/C, Cork [No.] 3 Brigade, and I had travelled a lot as I was in charge of the special services. There was not much good fighting in the Bantry area, but Tom Barry collared all our good arms, which went to the column; all our rifles.

IRB. I was centre of Bantry.[3] There was a circle in 1920, and I reorganised it in the Beara area. We had plenty of men for there was an everlasting supply of men for the column during the two wars, for the men were excellent. All the mountain areas and the poor areas were good.

Priests. The excommunication and the refusal to hear confessions, it had an effect. Only priests here and there took the risk of holding confessions and of going out to the column. The Proclamation had no effect on the fighting men.[4] At first,

---

2   The Ancient Order of Hibernians (AOH) is a Catholic political association founded in America in 1836. The group's aims are to support Irish independence and promote the Catholic faith; it has often been described as a 'Green' version of the Orange Order. In the early 1900s the AOH in Ireland was allied to John Redmond's Irish Parliamentary Party and used violence to silence political opponents and criticism of the party. There were frequent violent clashes between Irish Republicans and Hibernians during the Irish War of Independence, particularly in Ulster.

3   The lowest level of IRB organisation was a small group forming a cell called a centre, and the 'Centre' usually refers to the individual in charge of a cell, presumably what O'Sullivan means here.

4   This appears to refer to the Catholic bishops' denial of sacraments to IRA activists.

the more religious women were frightened, but in a month or so the effect wore off of them. Tom Barry did the most of his fighting in the eastern part of the brigade. Towards the end there were battalion columns as well, but by that time the enemy were also in stronger force, but by sniping and keeping the [2R] enemy on their toes. Barry had a 100 men and more in the Brigade Column.

Six Battalions. There was an average of 8 to 10 rifles in each battalion. Liam Deasy left for the Division to … there, the night before the Truce in July, 1921. He had been up to that Brigade O/C.

Brigade V/C Ted [O']Sullivan; Adj[utant]: Gibbs Ross.

Quartermaster: Tadg [O']Sullivan, who was a brother of Gearóid O'Sullivan, the Adjutant-General from Skibbereen.[5] As Brigade V/C, I swore in the men in the western area of the Brigade. I swore in 120 men in Skib[bereen] company, the only company where one man refused to take the oath, but he affirmed instead. Skib[bereen] was mostly Protestant and they stuck together better.

Spies: 3 or 4 were shot, but there were no spies in our ranks. We frightened people who were fraternising with the enemy.

Intelligence: It was very good in Bantry. Seán Buckley was Information Officer for the Brigade, and it was organised in each battalion. As it was a special service, it was under my

5 Here and elsewhere in the text quartermaster was abbreviated to Q.M. and adjutant-general to A/G.

control. The post office and railway passed on all information they received. The co[mpany] captain of Bantry Co[mpany] was in the post office there. Tommy Reidy was the Battalion Information Officer there. A … club in Bantry, second to none. He took lady searchers for a walk. He served also in the Civil War and he works in **[2L]** a hardware shop, Murphy O'Connor's, in Bandon. He is a North Kerryman.

Intelligence was despised in many areas (EOM: *for men thought of the fighting effort …, which was easy compared with the slow routine of sapping the enemy, being cautious and using their own as well as our sources. You would think that its cunning would appeal to the cunning in our race*). Collins had no influence in our area or Gearóid [O'Sullivan] in the Skibbereen area. Collins' area would have been Clonakilty, yet Gearóid's brother was with us in the Civil War.

(EOM: *Was Collins well-known to your men then?*) At Glandore Camp we first saw Collins. When reorganising Sinn Féin in 1917–1918 he came to the area. He just came to inspect the camp. Gearóid O'Sullivan visited us oftener. Seán Ó Muirthile came from a place a mile from Leap.[6] Our **[3R]** opinion was that he was a huge bluffer.[7] As an Irish organiser he first went to the Feisanna. As Adjutant General, all the

6   Seán Ó Muirthile was a top figure in the IRB. In the Civil War he served as quartermaster general in the National Army with the rank of lieutenant general.
7   In the original text here O'Malley has written big bluffer, but then added huge above the word big.

instructions we received came through the Adjutant General, Gearóid, as general orders.

Diarmuid O'Hegarty: he was from Schull side. He had no influence save what he might have had through his family.[8]

Our area was very well organised at the Truce.

Beara Island: was used by the British as a training ground.

Bantry and Skibbereen: had British troops. Bantry had the King's Own Liverpool Regiment, but they never ill-treated prisoners. We were able to obtain a continuous supply of communication through there by means of our Intelligence Officers and the Cumann na mBan.

The Essex Regiment were quartered in Bandon and Kinsale, and they were all bad to prisoners.

Bandon: was RIC Headquarters. There were a few RIC men fairly good, and Reidy was able to get around and to make contacts. Before the Truce there were a number of older Irish Volunteers and members of Sinn Féin who were not fighting men, and they beat us in accepting the Truce. We thought the Truce would last only a few weeks and we went hell for leather into it. We had brigade, battalion, and company camps, and a camp for the new members of the IRB. I swore **[3L]** no one in during the Truce. I swore in good key men whom you could depend on. We made no move in our area to reorganise the

---

8   Diarmuid O'Hegarty was a senior leader of both the military and political wings of the independence movement. His father, Diarmuid Ó hÉigeartuigh, was a teacher and prominent Gaelic League activist. Schull is incorrectly spelled Skull in the original text.

IRB during the Truce. The IRB of Bantry area, 30 men, went into training during the Truce.

We got an idea a few days before the Treaty was signed that the settlement was about to be made, but it was hearsay and we took no notice of it. Some time before this we got a wrinkle that we weren't being given a full [picture]. There was a reaction to de Valera's utterance in Thurles.[9] The Free State people used that a good deal as a lever. The terms came as a shock, but no fighting men accepted it. Then there was a campaign of priests and of constitutionalists and of course the fighting men were a small part of our population. There was no Free State post in our area, but **[4R]** there was an attempt in June [1922] to set up such a post in Skibbereen.[10] The Battalion O/C went Free State. Cornelius Connolly (Neilus) went Free State and most of his staff officers.[11] The first signs of organising was … in Collins' and Gearóid O'Sullivan's country. By that time Collins was a well-known figure, and we got a lot of 'What's good enough for Collins …'[12]

Skibbereen: A number of the maintenance party in Bantry Barracks walked out, for an ex-RIC man, MacCarthy of …

9   In March 1922 Éamon de Valera gave a controversial speech in Thurles, where he warned that opponents of the Anglo-Irish Treaty would 'wade through Irish blood' to achieve freedom.

10   Skibbereen is written as Skib here and elsewhere in the original text.

11   Cornelius 'Neilus' Connolly commanded the Skibbereen Battalion of the Cork No. 3 Brigade during the War of Independence.

12   A popular pro-Treaty saying at the time was: 'What's good enough for Michael Collins is good enough for me.'

was a training officer (now in Fermoy). He called them to attention, made them slope arms, and out they went. I was in charge of the barracks there. That was a stunt of the Provisional Government. The whole crowd of them went to Skibbereen, 40 or 45 of them. I had a Hotchkiss [machine] gun in the office, and I ran after it and it was dismantled in the office. They were organising the Free State Army at the time. They took on with Connolly in Skibbereen then, and they took over a house there as a barracks. Within a few hours I collected troops from another battalion, and I surrounded the house in Skibbereen.

Cork 3 [Brigade] area was divided in August of 1921 to form two brigades. From Crossbarry to the West was one brigade. The Kinsale area was a brigade.[13] Seán Lehane was in charge of Cork 3; Gibbs Ross was in charge of Cork 5 Brigade, and I was Vice O/C. Brigade Headquarters was in Bantry. This is why we had so many troops there. We surrounded the house in Skibbereen and they [4L] surrendered. I brought them back to Bantry in a lorry, and [let] them out gradually. ... Connolly held the RIC barracks in Skibbereen as a Free State post,[14] and the lads who remained Republican took a house at Liss[ard], Skibbereen, one mile from the town, so there was room for trouble. On the 1st of July [1922] there was no mobilisation.[15] No plan of action had been arranged for. We were more or less on our own.

13　This is incorrect. During the Civil War, the Kinsale area was not a brigade, but rather formed the 5th Battalion of the Cork No. 3 Brigade.
14　Neilus Connolly, who was head of the garrison there.
15　The start of hostilities after the attack on the Four Courts in Dublin.

Mossy Donegan and I were at a Convention in the Four Courts.[16] Seamus Robinson arrested me in the Four Courts.[17] We parked our car in the Four Courts, and when we returned Seamus Robinson placed us under arrest, and it was Dick Barrett who released us.[18] Dick Barrett was a quartermaster in [the] IRB, a district quartermaster.

Civil War: We had a dispatch on June 30th to say that the Republic had been attacked and to capture any Free State troops **[5R]** in our area. We attacked Skibbereen on July 1st and the Staters there defended it. We were starving them out. This went on for three days and in the end we got an old cannon from Killarney.[19]

Oliver Mason of Kerry One [Brigade] brought it over.[20] They had been working on it during the Truce, and they thought it was perfect but the damn thing weighed 7 or 8 hundredweight. It was mounted on two wheels of a donkey cart and we put it up to fire into the barracks about 30 yards away from us, under cover. There was a fellow killed beside … McCarthy, from Kilcoole on the 2nd of July.[21] We were 3 days on the attack.

---

16   Mossy Donegan, not Donovan as in the original text. There were three conventions, so it's not clear which one he's discussing.

17   Seamus Robinson was O/C of the Tipperary No. 3 Brigade and a member of the anti-Treaty IRA Executive. The date O'Sullivan was arrested is not known.

18   Dick Barrett was a colleague from Cork No. 3 Brigade.

19   This was a cannon seized by the IRA from Ross Castle in 1919. See *The Men Will Talk To Me: Kerry Interviews*, pp. 196–197.

20   Oliver Mason was a Volunteer officer from Killarney.

21   Section Commander Patrick McCarthy, not MacCarthy as in the original text.

There were cylinders pointed at one end and flat on the other end. This was the shell, 4 inches to a point, 2½ ..., packed with black powder which was put into the shell and there was a fuse. We packed sandbags on the wheels to take the recoil, and the bloody old thing blew back, and we didn't ever know where the shell went. But the gun made a great noise. There was a man of Seán Moylan's with Oliver Mason, and without doubt the gun made a wonderful noise.[22] Next day we put it in a house within 10 yards of the barracks and we let rip with the gun, and begod, the old shell went through the wall. We had to be very careful of shells. We made a few holes in the old barracks and they surrendered. T. [Barry?] has maps of his brigade area and also Liam [5L] Deasy, who also has a great deal of written material.

Posts vacated by the RIC: We had 2 companies from Kerry 2 [Brigade], Kenmare, Healy Pass, Ardreagh, and Laragh in Cork 5 [Brigade]. Healy Pass was 1st with Cork 3 [Brigade] after the Truce. There were 3 brigades in Cork during the Tan War and 5 after the Truce.

At the western end Beara

Allihies: Attacked and demolished, Feb[ruary] 1920.

Adrigole: They cleared out before " 1920.

Eyeries: Arms captured March 17, 1918.

22 Seán Moylan was leader of the Newmarket Battalion and later O/C of Cork No. 2 Brigade during the War of Independence. He fought on the Republican side in the Civil War. Some of Moylan's engineering officers had also experimented with an old brass cannon.

Martial law was declared and the troops were billeted in the village and kept there up to 1920, when they all cleared out both military and RIC.

The south side: the Bantry area. Kilcrohan, this was the first RIC post to be cleared out – at the end of 1919.

Durrus: An unsuccessful attack made in 1920. There **[6R]** was a hole made in the roof by which the men were to get in but they didn't get in. A few were wounded by a bomb and the RIC cleared out of it next day.[23]

Goleen, Mizen Head: They cleared out in April 1920. We raided Mizen Head for explosives, they cleared out next day.

Schull: An RIC man sold the password to Gibbs Ross and to Seán Lehane, and all the arms were captured.[24] Later on in 1920 they cleared out of it.

Baltimore: Cleared out in early 1920. Was burned September 1920.

Ballydehob: Cleared out before Schull, just as we were planning to attack it.

Only Skibbereen and Bantry were then held by the RIC.

Glengarriff: Only RIC in Castletownbere, but there were troops on Beara Island and a big camp at Furious Pier on the mainland.[25] Auxiliaries were put into Glengarriff to reinforce

---

23   This occurred on 28 March 1920.
24   Led by Seán Lehane, the Schull Battalion captured the Schull Barracks by stealth on 4 October 1920, capturing thirteen rifles and additional arms.
25   Furious pier, not Furris as in the original text.

Crown forces in Crossley tender lorries, Bandon Barracks, *c.* 1920–21.
(*Courtesy of Mercier Archive*)

A round-up of West Cork civilians by British troops, *c.* 1920–21.
(*Courtesy of Mercier Archive*)

Members of the 5th (Bantry) Battalion, Cork No. 3 Brigade, *c.* 1921.
(*Courtesy of Cork Museum*)

IRA suspects at Bandon Barracks.
(*Courtesy of Mercier Archive*)

A partially-destroyed bridge near Kinsale, West Cork.
(*Courtesy of Mercier Archive*)

RIC constables on patrol in West Cork.
(*Courtesy of Mercier Archive*)

Republican suspects in Bandon Barracks.
(*Courtesy of Mercier Archive*)

A British military lorry negotiates an IRA road trench.
(*Courtesy of Mercier Archive*)

Jim Hurley, Adjutant,
Cork No. 3 Brigade.
(*Courtesy of Cork
Museum*)

An IRA training camp in West Cork, date unknown.
(*Courtesy of Mercier Archive*)

Essex Regiment soldiers march
Republican suspects through
Bandon following the killing of
RIC Sergeant William Mulhern
in July 1920.
(*Courtesy of Mercier Archive*)

The bodies of unidentified Republicans in West Cork killed by members of the Essex Regiment.
(*Courtesy of Mercier Archive*)

A group of Republican prisoners in Hare Park Camp, 1924. Liam Deasy
appears to be seated in the second row, far left.
(*Courtesy of Cork Museum*)

the RIC. They took over the Eccles Hotel, and were, I think, 'C' or 'K' Company.

Castletownsend: RIC cleared it.

Drimoleague: held [by] RIC.

Glandore, Union Hall: Cleared out.

Leap: Cleared out.[26]

The Auxiliaries in Glengarriff were not bad. They rounded [up people?] … to fill in trenches. There were huge round ups from Beara Island to Furious Pier. Then [Royal Navy] sloops brought troops to the Kenmare River, but they were not a bad type like the Essex.

[6L] **Civil War:** Skibbereen Barracks had from 20 to 30 men. We had complete control of the area from 3rd July to the middle of August [1922]. The Free State crowd were quietly organising all the time. Skibbereen sent most men to Dublin to join the Free State Army. And they got good men in Skibbereen: Neilus Connolly, Mick [O']Donovan, a Kilmichael man, Jer McCarthy, a great soldier, the entire battalion staff in that area.[27] There was a good battalion commandant in Bantry who is now dead, Tom Ward.[28] They

26 Glandore and Leap in the original text were added in a white space on page 6L but have been moved here where they were probably originally intended to be included.
27 Michael 'MickLo' O'Donovan of Cullane, Leap, County Cork, partici-pated in numerous fights, including the Kilmichael Ambush. He served with the National Army during the Civil War. Jeremiah McCarthy, not MacCarthy as in the original text, was an active officer from Schull.
28 Tom Ward commanded the Bantry Battalion after Mossy Donegan's arrest in November 1920.

got others from the remaining areas but they were not worth much.

T[an] W[ar]: Tom Barry joined the IRA on the 31st July 1920. I can fix it by the photograph that was taken in Guy's.

Civil War: Brigade O/C Gibbs Ross, Adjutant: Michael Harrington, Vice Commandant: Tadg O'Sullivan, Quartermaster: Michael O'Callaghan. The present judge … general quartermaster, Harrington, resigned on the **[7R]** 1st of July and he was replaced by Michael Crowley of Castletownbere, who carried on until the end of the Civil War as adjutant. Free State troops landed at Glandore and Union Hall where we had a small outpost as coast watchers.[29] They cleared them out and they retreated to Leap, and the Free State came to Skibbereen. We rushed troops down, but they had already reached Skibbereen by moving across country for 5 miles, but it had been organised by the Free State before this. This was a strongly Free State area and our friends there were very few.

There were rumours of further landings along the coast, which didn't take place. We left a small party to hold Skibbereen, and we tried to hold off further landings. Their organisers went around, and in the 3rd week of August they came to Skibbereen with plenty of arms [and] the local fellows and they occupied the town.

---

29   Glandore, not Glendore as in the original text. In the early morning of 8 August 1922, 180 troops landed at Union Hall, while approximately 700 more landed at Passage West and Youghal.

Gibbs Ross, the brigadier, had never been in charge of a column. He had been formerly Adjutant to Cork 3. I was acting O/C of Cork 3. Tom Barry objected to my being made Brigade O/C, so Gibbs Ross, who was a cousin of mine, was appointed. Gibbs Ross had not handled men in the Tan War.[30] Mossy Donegan was second in command to me of the column, and we used to go into Bantry and upset the Free State there at night. Gibbs Ross was touring the brigade area whilst Mossy and I were planning [7L] how best we could capture Bantry.[31] On 30th August we mobilised all our men for an attack for they couldn't up to this show their noses (EOM: *outside their posts*). Poor Gibbs came along after us, and I told him how our men were distributed around. We had roughly 90 men. Between them at a reach, we would have had about 120 all told. We captured their first few billets about daybreak. We had taken about 8 or 10 billets and we ran into the flat of the town where Gibbs stood at the door of a billet and was shot through the head from the top windows of a house 250 [yards] away. It was more or less a stray bullet.

Donal McCarthy was hit from the same spot and Paddy Cooney of Dundalk, who had been working in Skibbereen, was killed on the other side of the town and within a half an hour,

30 He was primarily a staff officer, with the rank of brigade adjutant at the time of the Truce.
31 The Cork No. 5 Brigade attacked Bantry (rather than Bandon as in the original text) on 30 August 1922. O'Malley must have misheard or incorrectly transcribed the town name.

Michael Crowley was killed in the same spot again.[32] When [8R] Donovan's section joined me we captured more billets, but on account of the 4 lads dying being anointed we decided to retreat.[33] We had captured 22 prisoners with their rifles and ammunition. We had intended to remain in town until it was captured, and we wanted then to take the dead home.

The following week, the first week in September, the Free S[tate] came down and we had a meeting of the Brigade Council, and I was elected and was appointed O/C [of] the Brigade.

There were no peace moves in the area.

Liam Deasy came next day to bury Gibbs Ross. We released our prisoners on condition that they would not take up arms against us again, and they went home. The Free State were reinforced in Bantry from the sea, and from Cork through Clonakilty. We cut their communications in the towns, and we isolated them as much as we could. They organised the civil population, and everything we wanted, we had to commandeer. We burned all our barracks before we cleared out so that the Free State had to billet their men around the town. (EOM: *This procedure made them weaker in such an area as West Cork,*

32   The attack on 30 August cost the lives of Commandant Gibbs Ross of Bantry, Captain Patrick Cooney of Skibbereen (not Corry as in the original text), Lt Donal McCarthy of Ballydehob (not MacCarthy as in the original text) and Lt Michael Crowley of Glandore.

33   It would appear they decided to retreat to secure the Catholic sacrament of the Last Rites for the mortally wounded Volunteers.

which could operate at time[s] by surprise, isolating billets from each other, but in weaker areas the Free State who were not being attacked in the towns were evolving an intelligence system which could [8L] *either cooperate with the people in case of attack, or seize on the information which individual soldiers would possess.)*

Our brigade headquarters was between Keimaneigh and Bantry at Kealkil, which was also a battalion headquarters and a retreating ground for us in the Tan War. There was a good company there, and there were great people.

Tom Barry was watched day and night whilst he was helping at training in the Tan War. That is at the beginning of his training. ... I went into Cork to meet him and whilst ... interviewed him I kept gunmen on the door of the hotel with 2 revolvers. Then ... met his cousin ... who was killed later on, and then all three went to Guy's and had their photographs taken so that the photograph would date our first contact with Tom Barry.

[9R] **Truce 1922.** For the exchange of rifles you had better see Liam Deasy, for he had to do with the proposed attack on the North.

During the Truce and after the British had left our area the scheme for the exchange of arms was put up to me by Liam Deasy. I think he was to supply a certain number of men and rifles for action in the North, and the rifles to be exchanged were the rifles which we had captured from the British (EOM: *or been bought from them during the Tan War. These would include*

British military, RIC, Auxiliaries, Tans, and Coast Guard stations.
These rifles were to be exchanged at the barracks headquarters of
the Provisional Government, which was either Beggar's Bush or
Portobello, but those of the exchanges took place at Portobello.) Seán
Lehane was to take charge of the party which was to go up to
the north. He was a Brigade O/C of Cork 3 and we supplied
him with both men and rifles. 6 men: Billy [O']Sullivan, Tim
[O']Sullivan, John Murphy, Jack Fitzgerald, ... and a Crossley
tender ... from our area, which tender we had purchased
from the British who were allowed to sell all their gear and a
syndicate was to buy and distribute the stuff, and we took the
tender from the syndicate. The 1st Southern Division gave us
rifles in exchange. Jim Lane of Clonakilty was also with them.[34]
All of these men were up there until the Civil War began. He
was in Drumboe when the others were there. **[9L]** The 4 of
them, including Charlie Daly, were executed.[35] He [Jim Lane]
went a little queer then, and he is a little queer still. Billy [O']
Sullivan, who was captured later and escaped from Tintown
Camp.

[Tom] Kilcoyne of Dublin was in charge of the Free State
in Bantry.[36] He was a decent man. He did send a few men

34   Jim Lane was the engineering officer for the Clonakilty Battalion, Cork
      No. 3 Brigade, in the War of Independence, and joined other Cork officers
      in Donegal during the Civil War.
35   Seán Larkin, O/C of Tyrone No. 3 Brigade, Charlie Daly, Dan Enright
      and Tim O'Sullivan were executed at Drumboe Castle in March 1923.
36   Commandant Tom Kilcoyne, a member of Michael Collins' 'Squad'
      during the War of Independence, featured prominently in the National

from Bantry to contact me about peace at times, but I knew nothing about any peace moves and I told him I didn't know anything and that I would not deal with him.

Up to close on Christmas of 1922 there was no other Free State post in our area save Bantry and Skibbereen. We had a good column and we raided these towns at times and they sallied out, but we beat hell out of them each time they came out. A lot of ammunition was used for they had to fly back again. There were no troops in the area. All roads were cut by us and provisions were scarce in the houses. We commandeered a boat of flour in Castletownbere and we took cattle **[10R]** from the big shots. There was no man executed from our area, and no man from Cork 3 except Dick Barrett, but Cork 3 fell asunder quickly. There was no real brigade column to hold them, and the Free State had the towns around them held. Towards Dec[ember] they occupied Castletownbere, and they always recruited local fellows to guide them.

8th Dec[ember 1922]: the column was from 96 to 120 men. We had 3 machine guns, 1 Hotchkiss, and 2 Lewis, which we got from the Division during the Truce. Kerry 2 was under J. J. Rice [and] were masters of the situation.[37] We had complete control of the country. Moylan's report after his return from the USA[38] and there were accounts of each brigade given by the

Army's invasion of Cork in August 1922.

37 John Joe Rice was O/C of the Kerry No. 2 Brigade in 1922.
38 Presumably he is referring to Seán Moylan's trip to America from late 1922 to spring 1923 to raise money for Republicans.

brigade O/C to the Division. Our report showed the condition of our area at the time.

Coolea, Moynihan's of Ballyvourney, was a First Southern Division meeting. This was held in January (2) 1923.

Moylan went to Castletownbere by boat and he came back by … and his report was there at the Divisional Council when I was captured. I had reason to remember it for at that time the Staters were giving us the full whack. I had said that if John J. Rice and the other areas in Kerry and in Cork 1, 2, [and] 3 brigades didn't work harder I could not hold out. 'Now we'll intensify the war for you,' they said as they beat me.

The Divisional Headquarters was captured in [Tom] Crofts' time.[39]

8th Dec[ember]: our column was billeted in a line twice. **[10L]** The first billets were 1 mile away from Bantry on the north bank of the … and at half 7 the first sentry was shot. He died afterwards of his wound. I got out of bed with Mossy Donegan after the capture of the Slieve na mBan in Bandon, which was captured by Cork 3. McPeake gave it away.[40] They

39   Tom Crofts succeeded Liam Deasy as O/C of the 1st Southern Division. His headquarters at Gougane Barra was captured in 1923.
40   John 'Jock' McPeake, incorrectly spelled MacPeak in the original text, was a Scotsman born to Irish immigrants in Glasgow. He served in the British Army and was jailed for smuggling guns for the IRA in 1921. McPeake was the gunner in the Sliabh na mBan (then called the Slievenamon) armoured car during the Béal na mBláth Ambush in which Michael Collins was killed in August 1922. He deserted to the IRA in December 1922, but was arrested in Glasgow and served a five-year prison sentence in Portlaoise. Following his release he returned to Scotland.

were trying hard to get the armoured car, the Staters, and we had to take it the previous Sunday to see if we could get it into Bantry, but it used to sink in the roadway. As we had broken down all the bridges we could not get it into the town. We had an armoured lorry also, which came from Cork 1. Cork 1 took the armoured car away again and they took Ballyvourney with it.[41] But they left us the armoured lorry. We had a good position and we thought we had only a few troops to deal with. They pasted at us from across the river and Mossy went off to get the armoured lorry and with it get close to them. He drove through our position but saw [11R] nobody and then they got their armoured cars across the river, and Mossy, who didn't know they were there, went after them and they got another car in behind him. Mossy didn't know they were there and they didn't know that Mossy was there. They turned off to get behind us at Kealkil and he went on, and the second car turned off.[42] He drove off to a broken bridge where he found Drimoleague troops around him, so he set fire to the engine and he hopped it across to us. We had 8 sections and they were in a good position. We forced them back across the river and then more men came against us. They landed from off a boat at Ballylickey and they came up behind us. Dunmanway, Bantry, Drimoleague, and the ones who came in behind us

41   On 6 December 1922 IRA troops captured the National Army garrison at Ballyvourney, after a three-hour battle in which the Free State forces suffered numerous casualties.

42   Kealkil (here and following), not Keakle as in the original text.

from Kinsale and Cork to converge on Kealkil, looking for the Slieve na mBan. We didn't know what number they had there, but later we found that 2,000 men had surrounded us with 8 armoured vehicles to look for the Slieve na mBan.[43]

George Dease was killed first, the sentry, and in the evening a young chap, Seán Dwyer, in the 1st section near Bantry town.[44] We fought from 7 o'clock until 3, and at 3 I found they were all around us, but in front we were safe. We withdrew section by section across the mountain. There was a report that 21 of them were knocked out on all fronts.[45] We were at our ease then, and at dark [11L] they all withdrew to their bases again. They were to keep up that round up until they found the armoured car, and they found it three days later at Gougane [Barra]. Three men had McPeake for safety there [and] we got him to Kilgarvan and then to Scotland.

I divided the column into four sections:

1 to Castletownbere to harry the Free Staters

2 to Castledonovan near Drimoleague

3 to Skibbereen

4 with me, went to Ballydehob side, and I was in charge of it. The troops went back to their bases after a few days, and again we were able to keep our local garrisons within in [sic]

---

43 This may have been an overstatement, though the National Army did report a convergence on Kealkil by multiple columns deployed from military posts in Clonakilty, Kinsale, Skibbereen, Ballineen and Bantry.
44 George Dease of Castlehaven and John Dwyer of Castletownbere.
45 This appears to be another exaggeration.

the towns. We remained like that then, and there were isolated captures of men up to the 'Cease Fire'. Kealkil was only raided twice, although it is 6 miles from Bantry.[46] They only reached our headquarters twice.

[12R] We dumped our arms and we ran through the country, and they caught men wholesale.[47] Up to that time they had taken a lot of our combatants and they had filled the gaols with them. Wherever we'd camp today in 3s or 4s, they'd camp tomorrow. Mossy [Donegan] and two of the lads went into Bantry and they stayed there. I had the Brigade Adjutant and the Assistant Adjutant. The people were very good, but we had no money and we got no money sent out to us, so we commandeered cig[arette]s and clothes. The C[umann] na mBan knitted socks and gave us cig[arette]s. Only one man, a deserter who joined us, went back to the Free State, but in spite of bad grub and the lack of clothes, our men stayed on. Only one of our men handed up a rifle after the 'Cease Fire', but there was a wholesale handing up of rifles in other areas.

I was then Enemy No. 1, for they had never beaten me in the field. They put a column out after me. 'Evade arrest' was our order, but we should have marched in in a body after we had dumped our arms.[48]

Late in the evening of the 1st of June [1923] they got

46   Bantry (here and following), not Bandon as in the original text.
47   He is referring either to the period after the IRA's ceasefire order of 23 April 1923, or the 'Dump Arms' order of 24 May.
48   By marched in he means surrendered.

me. They brought me to Castletownbere town. I was put in a guardroom there, and at 3 o'clock in the morning, Frank O'Friel, a Dublin man in charge of the troops in Bantry, burst in the door of the guardroom flanked by Jim Hannon of Clare, one-eyed, and 3 other officers.[49] Ryan of Tipp[erary], now dead, one of them, shot himself in Bantry afterwards.[50] **[12L]** There were 3 prisoners there with me. I had my boots and my gaiters off and I had knickers and a shirt on. Frank [O']F[riel] had a bottle of whiskey in one hand, which was ¾ full, and a hammer in the other hand. He called for the prisoners, and we were in a corner of the guardroom lying down and the guards were present. He hit me with the hammer on the left side of the forehead and I went down. The mark is yet there. I stood up again, and I got a strike of a rifle held by the foresight, a full whack of it, from Jim Hannon, on the left side of the face and down I went.[51] I stood up again to get a stroke of a rifle by Hannon on the other side of the head, which he held by the magazine to make it shorter this time. I was still conscious but I was bleeding from the two ears. I am deaf even now when there is more than one person speaking to me. **[13R]** Hannon

49   Commandant Frank O'Friel, not Freal as in the original text, who had distinguished himself during the National Army's landing at Passage West.

50   Ryan of Tipperary cannot be identified. Another who shot himself was Captain John Stanley of Dublin.

51   Jim Hannon served in East Clare during the War of Independence and later rose to the rank of colonel in the National Army. He commanded the army's 1st Infantry Brigade at Collins Barracks, Cork, and was prominent in horse racing and clay pigeon shooting circles.

dropped the rifle and the two of them got around me. O'Friel continued to beat me with the hammer, but not too much as he was well drunk and the last I remember is Hannon having a hold of me by the testicles, threatening to twist them off me and O'Friel gave me another flake of the hammer. I went for O'Friel and I had him by the throat when the sergeant major of the guard, and ex-Irish Guardsman, waded in to save O'Friel and he hit me with his fist under the jaw and he put me out for good.

I remembered no more for a week. Edward [Ned] Cotter of Bantry, a County Councillor, was a prisoner. Patrick Mahoney, Ardgroom, and Patrick Crowley of Ardgroom were present when I was beaten up. They were looking on all the time. When the sergeant major hit me, O'Friel kicked me around and when I didn't move, he put whiskey back on me. O'Friel opened my mouth and said, 'put it back on him', and then I got up. I stood up and O'Friel and Hannon continued to beat me between the two of them, whilst Ryan was trying to save me. They left me for dead at 7 and they went off to bed. ... He was interned in Ballykinlar in the Tan War, a tall fair chap.

They returned at 7. I was able to stand and to walk, but I was quite foolish [concussed] and I was placed in the back seat of a car, a touring car with O'Friel on one side and Ryan on the other side. The other [13L] 3 men [were] put in a Crossley tender behind me on the way to Bantry. The prisoners in the lorry had a sight of the touring car and at intervals they could see O'Friel beating me with a stick, a short stick, and Ryan having his arms around my head trying to ward off the blows. When I got to Glengarriff I was taken out of the car and I was knocked and beaten publicly. No one interfered there. In Bantry town I was again taken out in the square parade, foolish as I was, like a goose with my head hanging and swaying, bleeding from the ears. I was crowned with a crown of laurel, my shirt was torn off, all covered as it was with blood, and I was publicly kicked and beaten.[52] The people booed the soldiers and they shouted. People protested then. I was brought to Bantry Barracks where I was placed in an outhouse where there were 20 of our men prisoners. I could walk and talk but I did not know **[14R]** anyone, and those present were my own men with whom I had been with [*sic*]. I was foolish and quiet, and I would ask a lad what was his name. The first thing I remember is Fr Vincent Hurley of Bantry, who defied the sentry and who came in to see me. He had been alright in both Tan War and Civil War. He had told the people of Bantry from the altar what he had seen, and he didn't get a parish until late in life, and he died soon afterwards. 'Go down on your knees,' he said, as if I was going to confession to him. 'I'll see that your people know about this,' he said. A military doctor came to see me, a doctor attached to the troops in Bantry. He examined me. My ears were running. I was battered black all over. He said

---

52   Billy O'Sullivan records the same episode in his interview (see p. 68).

nothing, and a week later I was taken to Cork Gaol. [Thomas] Nagle, TD, put a question in the Dáil as to why I had been ill-treated.[53] Cosgrave said: 'the prisoner attempted to escape, but there was no ill-treatment.'[54] I was taken up to an inquiry in Cork Barracks. O'Friel and Hannon and the doctor were present and they gave evidence and swore there had been no ill-treatment, but that O'Friel gave me a few flakes in an attempt to extract information.

'What's the good of making a statement,' I said. A doctor now in England, two weeks after the hammering, called in, Dr O'Driscoll, a West Cork man, and his brother who had been with us. 'No it would be as **[14L]** much as my job is worth, to say a word against that man.'

'Can you do anything for this man?' our man asked.

I was in Cork for a month, then I was sent to Mountjoy. O'Friel's brother, Henry O'Friel, had been secretary to Kevin O'Higgins.[55]

We went to Mountjoy on the 12th of September [1923] to C Wing, and I was placed (you were on the second landing), and I was on the top landing. Frank Barrett, Pax Whelan, and I went to you [EOM] and one of the things used against

---

53   Thomas Nagle, a leader of the Irish Transport and General Workers' Union, represented Cork city.
54   See *Dáil Éireann Debate*, Vol. 3, No. 32, Friday, 22 June 1923, p. 7. William T. Cosgrave was President of the Executive Council in the Dáil.
55   Henry O'Friel, Frank's older brother, was secretary to the Department of Home Affairs (later Department of Justice) from 1922 to 1933.

the hunger strike was that it would kill you.[56] You were very low at that time. You said you would go on hunger strike if it began. You didn't give a damn. And I'm sure we started on 13th October. You told us 'not to stop the hunger strike on my [EOM's] account'.[57] There was a canvass made from cell to cell. I don't know who started it. The men who came on it asked the fellows in each cell 'yes' or 'no' for **[15R]** going on hunger strike.

The row was on when we went into the thing. We got a lecture from Hughes of Dundalk when he got in the gate of Mountjoy.[58] 'Aren't you the f— that shot Michael Collins,' he said, and he threatened us what he wouldn't do with us. There were 3 or 4 of us in a cell down in the basement. 60 of us came up from Cork. We had no blankets and no beds but the floors were not bad at all, so we just sat down. After a few days we got blankets and a spoon, a knife and fork each and we were marched into the wing by a side door, and all the lads in B Wing looking down on us. This was the 1st of September and there were no cells occupied on the ground floor. 'Get in to your cells,' was the order, and the lads above were waiting to tell us not to carry out any of the prison orders. They were after clearing out the ground floor men with the hose.[59]

---

56   Frank Barrett of Mid-Clare served on the IRA Executive; Pax Whelan was a senior IRA commander from Waterford in the War of Independence and Civil War.

57   Ernie O'Malley was very badly wounded during his capture, and his fellow prisoners apparently feared he would not survive.

58   Captain Patrick Hughes was deputy military governor of Mountjoy.

59   Liam Deasy may have referred to the same incident. See his interview, p. 197.

In they came with the hose in the morning. 'Get out,' they shouted, and they wanted us to go to work. But the fellows above shouted to us not to go out for them. They hosed us out of our cells, but the fellows on top had not a proper force of water at all. We were put out in the compound and we were all wet. The hose was strong enough to knock you if were not against a wall. There were 7 or 8 of us in the cells above. We left the ground floor alone. **[15L]** We divided our cig[arette]s amongst each other. Every fourth day we were put out. The PAs were very good there.[60] Fitzpatrick used a walking stick one day on poor old Seán Buckley outside in the compound.[61] You could see the steam rising off our clothes. We had no parcels, no letters, no papers, no cigarettes, and the fellows were getting desperate. The sentry would give warning and let off a banging, and the banging there was terrible.

They came for me 3 or 4 times at night to shift me to Kilmainham, but I wouldn't give my name and on the 7th of January [1924] we went to the Curragh. Our beds and blankets in Hare Park Camp had been left out in the rain for a day inside the camp gate and so were very thoroughly wetted. There was a fire in the middle of every hut. It was very frosty and the huts had been fairly well wrecked for asbestos sheeting had been once inside **[16R]** the galvanised sheeting and our blankets were stiff with frost.

---

60   A PA (Póilíní Airm) is a military policeman.
61   Seán Buckley was an intelligence officer in the Cork No. 3 Brigade and later a longtime Fianna Fáil TD representing West Cork. No information was available on the identity of Fitzpatrick.

In Hare Park on the previous day a trench had been dug by forced labour and it had been dug when we arrived.

[Dick] Hume had died of … in hospital and I had been ill since January from …[62] Poor Jack Keogh used to steal a bit of meat for me out of the butchers shop and make beef tea for me, for with the p[neumonia] I could not eat.[63] The inquest which was held on Hume in Wexford said that he had died of neglect, and on the night of the inquest I had visits from 7 different officers, for I couldn't eat and my gums covered my teeth. I refused to go to hospital, but I was taken off.

Peter Hegarty was suffering from neglect in the heels. Mark W… for varicose veins; Paddy Quinn's thigh was not thicker than your finger.[64] Your uniform for escape they found in a hole over the lavatory, and I had the bed next to the lavatory. A medical orderly was dusting the ceiling when he found the trap door. You [EOM] were still there behind and I suppose they suspected that the uniform was for me, for you could not walk. A Sergeant Daly who was bringing me to the Curragh said, 'You won't get out of here me lad.'

Corcoran who gave a blood transfusion [16L] to Hume never got over it for he was sickly himself afterwards. Jerry

---

62   Dick Hume, a former member of the North Wexford Flying Column, died in hospital on 9 November 1923.

63   Jack Keogh was an active officer in the Galway anti-Treaty IRA, based in Ballinasloe. His commitment to Dundrum mental asylum allegedly resulted from abusive treatment he received in prison. He escaped from Dundrum in 1926. See *Dáil Éireann Debate*, Vol. 15, No. 3, p. 11, 22 April 1926.

64   No information could be found about these men.

O'Grady, a solicitor from N[orth] Tipp[erary], from Nenagh, had sciatica.[65] He fell off a wall when he was escaping from Kilkenny Gaol and he injured his sciatic nerve. Corcoran was a Wexford man and there they paid great attention to me. But the doctors and the dentists were no good. Neglect in bed had injured Peter [Hegarty]'s heels.

Keogh was in a hut with me and we collected any cash the lads had in their shaving sticks to buy the stuff for Keogh's escape.[66] He was to get along under the huts nearest to the gate, waiting for a certain man to get in touch with him at night, but nothing happened. There were attempts to buy off the rubbish man who brought out stuff from the workhouse in a horse and butt, but he **[17R]** wouldn't. And in the end Keogh decided to go out in the waggon that brought out the blankets, but some authority decided that he would be suffocated. Keogh was a wild lad in East Galway, and all he did wasn't according to schedule. There was a lot of agitation about the release of prisoners in the Dáil from the Labour men, and Kevin O'Higgins always quoted Keogh. He said he wouldn't be released and he used him as a sample of the prisoner type.

Peadar O'Donnell got a uniform off a Northern man, Doherty the PA, and the next thing was that Peadar walked out and left Keogh behind. Keogh was sentenced to 20 years

65   No information could be found about O'Grady.
66   For another version of Keogh's escape, see *The Men Will Talk To Me: Galway Interviews* (Cork, 2013), pp. 244–246, 249–250.

on two charges. He gave tongue to the judge. 'I'll be a free man, and you can look out then.' He was supposed to be insane later. They used hot irons and needles and everything on him as tests, but he stuck out all the tests and they brought him to Dundrum Asylum. (EOM: *Mrs Bob Brennan was afraid of Keogh when he was in the house for he was certainly mad, she said.*)[67]

There was a clause in some employment scheme by which our released prisoners or IRA men could not be employed until all ex-Free State soldiers had been employed. All the LGB officials had to take an oath of allegiance.[68] Technical and vocational teachers had to take an oath of allegiance. The oath **[17L]** was required for a government or a semi-government job. Dispensary doctors had also to take the oath.

Dan Holland of Timoleague was O/C of Cork 3rd Brigade during the Civil War. He's a sound, sensitive, good man and he owns a pub and a farm.

IRB August 1917:

Dumps: We used sewer pipes 10 to 12 inches long and joined together and they were stuck into cross sections of fences.[69] The pipes were 6 feet long. We used a bank, placing our pipes there so that they could be located and also be easily

---

67   Una (Anastasia) Brennan was the wife of Robert (Bob) Brennan, editor of the *Irish Bulletin* Republican propaganda newspaper, writer, journalist and Irish diplomat.

68   LGB = Local Government Board.

69   The original text has an extra they in this sentence: And they they were stuck.

accessible.[70] We used concrete dumps underground. My father's place was raided and searched 100 times, and no one ever came across the dump until in 1925 the CID and the Guards came on it. Usually we selected a field which was higher than the field below it so that whatever **[18R]** was hidden could be got at from the outside. Most of the officers had such dumps, and the earthenware pipes were a perfect job.

Dugouts: We had very few. One used by our relatives during the terror was in a corner of a field, and consisted of a couple of sheets of corrugated iron covered with furze and earth. We could not make dugouts in West Cork for the ground was too stony. We used caves and holes under big rocks. Plumis = hole under a rock.

Towards the end of the Tan War huge dumps were made out of 1½ inch planks, which were to hold from 20 to 30 rifles. The arms were to have been landed at Union Hall. [Liam] Deasy has all this planning in detail. These special dumps were in connection with the arms landing from Italy.[71] We made these dumps in every company area but they were captured in the Civil War. After the 'Cease Fire' the lads made their own

70   In the original text there is a very basic diagram added by O'Malley to illustrate this after the word bank.
71   In 1921, under pressure from the Cork brigades to supply weapons, IRA GHQ arranged an ill-fated arms smuggling operation in Italy. Mick Leahy, vice-commander of the Cork No. 1 Brigade, travelled to Genoa, Italy, to arrange the shipment, but purchasing funds never arrived from Michael Collins. The scheme may have been uncovered by British intelligence.

private dumps. In the roof [of] a farmhouse a space would be made above the collar beam, which was across to the rafters. A man could have room to lie there for a while.

T[an] W[ar]. Our battalion was attached to Cork 3 [Brigade] in January 6th [*sic*] 1919. I was appointed Battalion O/C by Michael Collins in August 1919 after the camp at Glandore. **[18L]** We had 6 rifles and 3 revolvers. Michael O'Callaghan was Battalion Quartermaster. He is a railway clerk and lives at 47 Booterstown Avenue, Blackrock. He is a B.L [Barrister at Law].[72] A few half ones and he'll talk. He was Brigade Quartermaster in the Civil War. There was a couple of tons of guncotton which had been stolen in rowing boats and then buried. Then they tried to exchange it for arms, as the guncotton was lying idle. So Michael Collins wrote me a personal letter asking for the guncotton. It was sent up to GHQ, but it was pilfered on the way up. 20 boxes of guncotton, not even half a cwt in each box.[73]

We had explosives and electric detonators. The slabs were hard to explode for they needed a dry primer, and we lost a lot of it, for it didn't go off.

All the dry guncotton came from the Fastnet Light and the light houses.[74] In our first raid on Mizen Head we **[19R]**

72   It is unclear what BL stands for. O'Sullivan is saying that Michael O'Callaghan will open up to O'Malley if he is provided with sufficient drink.

73   cwt = hundredweight.

74   The West Cork IRA conducted a series of raids on lighthouses to secure guncotton (written as g/c in some cases in the original text) used to sound fog cannons. The most famous was the daring raid in June 1921 on the Fastnet lighthouse, off Cape Clear Island.

captured a ton and a half of it. On the second raid we got 15 cwt. Later on we got a ton of it on a boat from Fastnet. This was used in mines so that we could use them in ambushes.

The Tans shot a young fellow dead in Bantry, a cripple named Crowley whose brother was in the Volunteers, and they attempted to burn a house.[75]

Beara: They blew up 4 houses. Pronsias O'Sullivan's house was one of them.[76] In 1921 we were to land arms in Kilmacalogue in Kerry, near Lauragh.[77] They would be rifles and trench mortars from Italy, and from the USA. I left it ... one evening to go over to arrange about the arms' landing and when I came back there was no trace of the house. It was a thatched house. What kind of explosive did the British use on this job? The house was destroyed as a reprisal for some of their soldiers who had been shot on the 4th of May.[78] There were 3 burning jobs on houses locally as well.

The British burned Murphy's of Snave, near where I shot an RIC man in Snave[79] who was named [King].

---

75 Cornelius Crowley's death on 25 June 1920 was one of many crown force reprisals, which were raised in parliament. See *Hansard*, HC Deb, 02 June 1921, Vol. 142, cc1213–4.

76 No information could be found on Pronsias O'Sullivan.

77 Lauragh, not Laragh as in the original text, is just over the Kerry border, on the Beara Peninsula.

78 O'Sullivan is probably referring to the IRA's killing of three British soldiers (members of the King's Own Scottish Borderers) on 14 May 1921.

79 On 12 June 1920 Constable Thomas King was shot dead at Snave Bridge, near Glengarriff.

Sullivan's near Ballydehob.

Yerra, it was easy to get away from the RIC. Our area was over 100 miles long.

[19L] Crookstown: I was coming from the Brigade Headquarters at Upton, and I was then responsible for the maintenance and movement of Brigade Headquarters. One day I was on a saddle horse, for we used to make use of a horse to a good extent. Bikes we used to commandeer, but they were soon used up. There was a good house belonging to a Mrs Keane in Crookst[own], and I went into it one day. I had left the horse outside the door. The Auxies from Macroom surrounded the house just as I got into it. They were at the front and at the back, three lorryloads of them. I had my Sam Brown[e] belt and my gun on me and what was I to do? There were tailors on the floor sitting down cross-legged, sewing away like hell. I went up and I whipped off my gun, and I sat there sewing like hell at an overcoat. My heart was out my mouth when they stood over me. I **[20R]** thought he was the biggest man in the world when he stood there, and he was a big man. 'F— Shinners,' he said. He asked each man his name and how long he was there and I hadn't even thought of a name. You, 'Taylor,' I said to him, and I thought he'd be able to hear my heart thumping. The officer came in then. 'Did you examine these f—?'

'Oh yes I did,' the Auxie said.

A little girl came into the shop, Kitty Cronin, and she came into the room. I was in the corner and she whispered to me,

'What's your name Ted?' and then I thought no more of her. The officer examined us again and I told him I was there since the burning of Cork. 'Were we f— Shinners?' No, we all denied our faith. 'Go down,' he said, 'and bring us the f— card from the back of the door and we'll soon see who they are,' he said. I could have got the two of them as they stood there, for my gun was under my backside on the floor.[80] The second man brought us the card and on it was Tom Taylor. Kitty had written it up without saying a word to anyone. And she was refused a pension and she is in hard circumstances now. In towns and villages they had the names of those in the house up on the back of the door. This was near Béal na mBláth (blossoms) where Collins was killed, but we didn't know he was killed until a few days [20L] afterwards.

If they saw a fellow passing they would report to us. During the Truce I met Michael Collins in Dublin and [at] 68 Parnell St, and Gearóid O'Sullivan, for they were there very frequently.[81] Collins drank whiskey. I saw Gearóid who was drinking a green drink and I asked him what it was and he said it was Chartreuse. From Kirwan's we went to the Salthill Hotel. They took me to the Abbey Theatre where I met Seán

---

80 In 1921 residents in martial law areas had to post a card on their front doors each evening, listing the names of everyone who could be found in the house.

81 Liam Devlin's Public House, an unofficial headquarters for Michael Collins.

MacEoin.[82] Gearóid and myself, [Liam] Devlin and Emmet Dalton, were kind of entertaining men.[83] Gearóid knew me very well, personally. There was a lot of poking fun there at that time, and it was done by Joe O'Reilly, who used to meet us during our [anti-Treaty] Army Conventions.[84] He seemed to be a scout for those lads. The Collins loyalty was a strange thing. They were drunk with power and with money,[85] but the loyalty of our men was a greater thing. We [21R] saw our own disorder then. Cathal Brugha was very impatient with the lads.[86] Joe O'Reilly was promising us jobs and money. He took us into Stephen's Green and he was trying to point out to us the advantages of the Treaty, and what they could do with the Treaty. They could control arms and they could control the country. What was good enough for Mick Collins would have been good enough for him, was his outlook.

Erskine Childers: We heard that Seán Ó Muirthile had assaulted Childers when he was a prisoner. Childers had a printing press in Cork 1 [Brigade] at Gougane Barra, and he moved back to Kealkil for a week or two. He had a horse and car and a few men to move his gear. He stayed at Ceappaghbue

82 Seán MacEoin, not MacKeown as in the original text, was an IRA commander from Longford, a general in the National Army and a longtime TD.

83 Emmet Dalton was a former officer in the British Army, the IRA director of training, and a major-general in the National Army.

84 Joe O'Reilly was a close aide of Michael Collins.

85 Money from Collins, as director of finance.

86 Cathal Brugha was Minister of Defence during the War of Independence and a top political leader in the Civil War split.

(Yellow Heights) in 3 or 4 houses, but principally Sweeney's and Mahony's. I was in charge of a column and I was away from the place and he would get his report from me of what was happening. He was very nice, gentle and understanding. He was a frail-looking man, full of sympathy for the lads if they had either bad boots or bad clothes. He moved off away from us then and we heard no more of him.

Executions: They had no effect on our fellows. Look up Jack Gwynne's articles in the *Manchester Guardian* for May of 1923, for he met me **[21L]** and he wrote a report of the situation.

It was hard to realise how brutal to us once-sincere Republicans were, and they paid for being brutal to us. We were threatened that more of our men would be shot if anything happened outside. The brutality was from the top. What could the hirelings below do?

Two lads, Patrick Mahoney and Patrick Crowley were taken back from Bantry again to Castletownbere and they were hammered with revolver butts in C[astletown]bere to get information from them, where our dumps were. They made the two of them dig their own graves. In 1924 in spring Crowley died. He had been a healthy young man and he was operated on in [the] head. It was after that that he died. The beating up fractured a bone in his head, or in his nose. Generally speaking, all prisoners were **[22R]** subjected to some kind of a hammering. I was 2 or 3 weeks in Cork Gaol when a gang came in who took me out to the office. They were supposed to be the intelligence gang. Lt Col Collins, a Corkman, was an awful bastard.[87] He had two others with him and he told me I was for it. I was getting over my hammering by this time. 'Well you can't do any more to me,' I said, 'than you have done.'

'Oh yes, we're going to take you out for a ride one night.' He asked me where the arms dumps were, and if I told him he said he would release me if I told him [*sic*] where the arms were. He tried to cajole me. I would be a very well-off man if I told him and I could return to private life. Then he began to threaten again about 'the ride'.

'I'm ready to go with you now,' I said.

'I'll will be back later tonight,' he said.

After our release the CID up to 1930 gave me a terrible time. They used to call at the house in Cork, arrest me, bring me to Union Quay, search me thoroughly, and they would look for dumps.[88] They used first to cajole, then threaten. They'd come in and sit down, codding and blackguarding you. One night they would go to the other lads and say that I sent them to give them rifles. They used to pretend at times that they were IRA looking for me. Once, in 1928, I was cutting turf in a bog [22L] when I got a telegram to meet the 10 train from Dublin to Cork, and it was signed 'Jack Martin', (who was

---

87   This appears to be Seán Collins Powell, nephew of Michael Collins, who rose to the rank of lieutenant general in the National Army.

88   Union Quay, a headquarters of An Garda Síochána.

married to Nora O'Brien, and he lives in Cork).[89] I wondered what he wanted me for. Anyway, I went to Cork and I was there at 11.30. When I went in, he said, 'You're very late.' I told him about my wire. 'They're on to', and there stood the CID, I thought. At 12.30 I found that they had been there in the area to call on the some of the lads to say that I had gone to meet the Dublin train and that we were to land a cargo of arms that night and that they were to have a boat ready when I came back from Cork. They got a lad to tell them where the boat was, and they wanted a few guns to have ready for me. Then this lad tumbled to what was up. He came to my wife and he told his **[23R]** story to her. She told him it was a CID stunt. They went to three different lads and he warned the other two lads.

I had cars for hire and they would search both cars and passengers (EOM: *this was a deliberate attempt to ruin his business and provoke an attack on them*). Reynolds was in charge of the raid for arms.[90] He had two prisoners, Harrington at Macroom and fined £30 … a Sergeant Reynolds but Gerry Boland would not sack him when he was Minister for Justice.[91]

C[ivil] War: One young lad executed, more or less unofficially, a boy in his teens named McCarthy. He used to

---

89   Jack Martin was a senior IRA figure in Cork city; Nora O'Brien was a leader of Cumann na mBan.

90   It is not known who Reynolds was.

91   Gerald 'Gerry' Boland, not Jerry as in the original text, was the brother of Harry Boland. He was active with the anti-Treaty forces in the Civil War and a senior figure in Fianna Fáil during his thirty-eight years in Dáil Éireann.

show the Free State the houses so that they could raid them so our lads shot him on Patrick's Day 1923 without sanction.[92] We used to issue proclamations.

The *Skibbereen Eagle* used to be there during the Civil War as the *Southern Star*, and very bitter it was.

In Stradbally there was a postman missing. He had been drinking in a pub in County Waterford and he was never heard of afterwards. It was supposed that he had been killed in the barracks. They used to hand in Republicans there and beat hell out of them. People there had to sit up and take notice and 4 or 5 Guards were dismissed.[93]

Ballads: 'We are the boys of the Third Cork Brigade'
            'The Boys of Kilmichael'.

Excommunication: There were no priests at [23L] burials from September 1922 onwards, so we buried our men ourselves.

Denis Kelly was surprised in a round up and he got away a few fields but he was destroyed by explosive bullets, one in the arm and another in the back, which made a huge hole in each case. [The] Free Staters had sent somebody for the priest but

---

92   The victim was sixteen-year-old James 'Benny' McCarthy (not MacCarthy as in the original text) of Ardra, Bantry, killed in March 1923. He was shot as part of a broader IRA reprisal for recent National Army executions of Republican prisoners.

93   Stradbally is in County Waterford, not Wexford as in the original text. Larry Griffin, the postman, disappeared on Christmas Day 1929. His body was never found and although it was assumed he had been murdered, no one was ever convicted. For more details, see Fachtna Ó Drisceoil, *The Missing Postman: What Really Happened to Larry Griffin?* (Cork, 2011).

the priest refused to come, the curate in Kealkil. The lad was dying.[94] The same curate refused to baptise the 11th child of a man who used to feed and harbour us. The father took the child into Bantry and it was baptised in the parish church of Bantry. We had cases of women being refused Absolution in confession unless they would promise not to harbour, feed or help their sons in any way when they came to their home. Well-known Republicans were passed over at the altar whenever they knelt there to [24R] receive Holy Communion. This had no effect on the people. A lady teacher who was Cumann na mBan and who had been with us in the Civil War was unemployed, for she wouldn't be allowed to teach or to substitute in any school in the Parish. She would have lost her profession had she not got a job in a Protestant school. Then she got a job as a teacher in the diocese of Kerry, and so she was able to follow her profession.

T[an] W[ar]: Tom Barry was in touch with the anti-Sinn Féin Society in Bandon, when he came home from the B[ritish] A[rmy]. This society in Bandon consisted of the Loyalists and the Essex Regiment. Barry brought up before the Board 3 men who had held no rank at the time, to prove that he, Barry, had been training men before he joined the I[rish] V[olunteer]s.[95]

94 Lt Denis Kelly of Bantry was killed on 17 April 1923 in Kealkil.
95 This refers to Barry's bitter dispute with the Military Service Pensions Board over the length and nature of his IRA service.

C[ivil] W[ar]: Barry had resigned officially. He had no rank. He said he was Deputy C[hief of] S[taff]. He called 2 or 3 meetings of the [1st Southern] Divisional Council to condemn Deasy for he hated Liam like hell. Deasy's letter was discussed by us at a Div. Council, but we refused to have anything to do with it.[96] Seán Buckley had stated that Barry had joined the Irish Volunteers in 1919, but this was wrong.

C[ivil] W[ar]: Did the Free State bomb or burn out Noel Hartnett's mother's place in Kenmare? Our fellows had done something to Dr Moore's daughters who used to associate with **[24L]** Free State officers in Kenmare.[97] There were 20 burnings in Cork 5 [Brigade] by either the Free Staters or ourselves.

Seán Hayes, governor of Newbridge … but he lived in Dublin.

Arms in Cork 3 Brigade at the end of the Tan War: 200 to 300 rifles, about 300 rifles, and a reasonable amount of stuff. There was a dribbling of stuff out of military barracks all over the place. We got plenty of ammunition, some rifles and revolvers. I don't know so much about Bandon, for the Essex were bitter for no one was associating with them. Daniel Minihane was the contractor for stout and whiskey to the military barracks to the mess. (EOM: *Every day he was in the barracks.*) He took terrible risks. Every day he got stuff out. In

---

96   Liam Deasy's surrender appeal to the IRA in January 1923.
97   Dr Moore had been hostile to the IRA during the War of Independence.

the end he had to bring away the very reliable soldier, and he brought his rifle and ammo out to **[25R]** Dan's place before the Truce. We had Patrick Sarsfield Brady and a Major de Barry, a retired Br[itish] officer, and Jasper Wolfe from Skibbereen, the retired Crown Solicitor. We had them [as] hostages up to the Truce for over a month, in case any of our fellows would be executed.[98] They were released at the Truce.

I took Jasper Wolfe again during the Civil War, about July 2nd, and we intended to shoot him. We occupied his house on the 1st of July to attack the Free State Barracks from it, but he hopped it and next morning in town at daybreak I was inspecting positions and he rolled into my arms. He was making his getaway and nobody saw him, Mossy Donegan and I agreed … Jasper prevailed on his sentry to take a note out for a half pint of whiskey for him, so that the Free State would know where he was. We released him that evening. The Free State tried some of our fellows for murder and he defended them free. There was one case of 'murder' in Bantry, and the Crown Prosecutor became Republican defendant; also … tried for robbery. He was a Protestant and a Britisher. At the same time we had taken prisoners of Sheehy and Swanton of the *Skibbereen Eagle*.[99] In Clonakilty and in Bandon the lads had

98   Jasper Wolfe's biographer reports that he was first kidnapped during the Truce period, in early October 1921, and again in early July 1922.
99   Edwin Swanton, a Skibbereen draper and supposed friend of Jasper Wolfe, was kidnapped, but escaped during the Truce period. Patrick Sheehy was editor of the *Skibbereen Eagle* newspaper.

a few prisoners about the same time and they were released at the Truce.[100]

Organisers from GHQ: Hugh Thornton was here for a time in 1919 and 1920.[101] He went around to companies and battalions.

[25L] Canon Duggan was chaplain to the Bon Secour nuns.

Rifles from GHQ: Dick Barrett did get some stuff from GHQ.[102] He was [Cork No. 3] Brigade Quartermaster up to the time he was arrested in May of 1921, and then Tadg [O']Sullivan was Quartermaster. We got these rifles before Barry came on to us. You had better see Liam Deasy about Barry's remark that no one in West Cork could take charge of a flying column.[103]

Seán Culhane of Cork was on the Swanzy job, but he's a peculiar fellow.[104] Dick Murphy and Sandow were on this job as well.[105]

---

100 These were the Earl of Bandon, Charles Sealy King, John James Fitzpatrick and John St Leger Gillman.

101 Hugh Thornton acted as an organiser for IRA GHQ, served as a staff officer in the brigade, and was killed by the IRA in Clonakilty while in command of National Army troops in the Civil War. His brother Frank was closely associated with Michael Collins.

102 Dick Barrett was later executed by the Irish Free State as a reprisal for the IRA's assassination of Seán Hales, TD.

103 In *Guerilla Days in Ireland* (p. 25), Tom Barry wrote that no member of the brigade staff was willing, 'to undertake responsibility of taking command of the Brigade Flying Column'.

104 District Inspector Oswald Swanzy was assassinated in Lisburn, County Antrim, on 22 August 1920 by members of the Cork No. 1 and Belfast brigades. Swanzy had been blamed for the killing of Lord Mayor Tomás MacCurtain the previous March. Swanzy's killing triggered extensive anti-Catholic riots in the town.

105 Dick Murphy, active in the Cork city IRA, accompanied Seán Culhane to

We thought we could manufacture a gas. There was a dispensary doctor, Michael MacCarthy, who had been a medical officer in the British Army, who was our brigade medical officer, then battalion medical officer.[106] He was at Durrus and he was sure he could make gas. We raided Cork G[reat] S[outhern] Railway and we took away two of these gas containers to Bantry. Raymond Kennedy and his brother we got in touch with.[107] The doctor tried to make a gas but he failed for want **[26R]** of ingredients. We thought we could make a gas that would put the enemy asleep. He lived two doors away from the RIC Barracks and he was a first-class intelligence officer as well. That night we had only 6 rifles and 1 which had been taken off an RIC man in the battalion. At that time Durrus RIC Barracks had armoured plates and [was] protected with barbed wire. He told us that if we could get to the barracks by a certain time, he would keep the RIC drinking in Ross's pub and he could get the password from them, but when I got there they had gone to the barracks and the pub was closed.

I got in next door to the barracks with a sledgehammer. The barracks was higher than the roof I was on, but I climbed up on top, broke the slates with 3 … Seán Lehane and Tim Ward (Free Stater) were in the house next door with others, and they passed me up home-made bombs. I had two rather big ones

Lisburn, but Dan 'Sandow' O'Donovan did not.
106   Medical officer is shortened to M.O. in the original text.
107   Raymond Kennedy taught chemistry at University College Cork, while his brother Denis was a civil engineer.

made of metal piping, six inches in diameter, and 18 inches in length, filled with Plaster of Paris, scrap and gelignite. I got in the first one, and it made a terrible bloody bang and it blew the hand off one RIC man and severely wounded another. We had two rifles in front under Mossy Donegan and 2 rifles behind. I was sitting more or less on the gable. I lit the fuse of the second bomb, but the fuse came out and the bomb dropped down harmlessly. I had a supply of paint tins filled with gelignite and scrap. This was on 31st March [26L] 1920. I realised I couldn't get the police out, so I decided to burn down the bloody thing. We had 5 or 6 tins of petrol. I got the petrol up and I poured it in, but I poured it over myself as well, and my clothes got pulled off by the nails on the rafters. I set fire to the barracks and myself, and I had to keep up the racket with bombs. Someone in the barracks was calling for a doctor and I was calling on the police to come out and surrender. The old sergeant was willing to come out, but that night the RIC there had been reinforced by a blackguard from Bantry. Liam … had told me that the sergeant wasn't a bad fellow at all, that I wasn't to shoot him. At daybreak we left the barracks there blazing. We told the doctor to go in to the barracks. The RIC put out the petrol with sand. I should have mixed paraffin with the petrol, but I thought at one time the old barracks was burned out. Next day the [27L] RIC cleared into Bantry.

Liam Deasy was senior officer in Crossbarry, and it was he who directed the flanking movement. We always gave him the credit for Crossbarry, and it was his advice that was acted on that day.

Rosscarbery:[108] Barry wanted me to guard the Ross Road, but I refused. 'I'm not going to [do] it this time,' I said, for Tom Barry wanted to get me away from the action. I was then on the storming party and I decided I was going to be in there first on account of all I had suffered from that bastard, Tom Barry. I wanted him not to put the place on fire, and to allow us to charge across after the explosion, but he told the men in the windows to open fire and after a while the police had steadied themselves from the shock of the explosion. The setting of the barracks on fire meant that we could not capture the arms.

There were 44 rifles available for the column, leaving a few rifles in each battalion area for local work. South of Bandon was good land and bad people, and w[est] of Bandon were good people and bad land.

Tom Barry's father was in the RIC and once he used to escort Judge O'Donnell of the Pension's Board. Barry of course reminded O'Donnell of this and they became friends as a result.

---

108 The attack on Rosscarbery Barracks occurred on the night of 30–31 March 1921.

FLORRY BEGLEY

(UCDA P17b/111, pp. 49–54)[1]

Florence 'Florry' Begley (1898–1979) was born in Bandon, joined the Irish Volunteers before the Easter Rising, and became a valued staff officer in the Cork No. 3 Brigade. He fought at the Upton Ambush, and was closely associated with brigade commanders Charlie Hurley and Liam Deasy. A noted musician, Begley won the lifelong moniker 'Piper of Crossbarry' for playing his pipes during the Crossbarry Ambush. During the Civil War he fought on the Republican side, before returning to Bandon. His newsagent shop on Main Street became a favoured meeting place for passing IRA veterans. In later years Begley organised military pension material for the 'Old IRA' and participated in numerous Republican commemorations. He was active in both Fianna Fáil and the GAA, and died in 1979.

***

1   Begley submitted two witness statements to the BMH – WS 32 and WS 1771.

(*EOM: Bandon, written next day for Florry did not like my note taking.*)

[49R] [Patrick] Coakley the spy:[2] For a month or two he wasn't at home although he was not even on the run for he was avoiding IRA duties as well as avoiding the British. He did not answer battalion queries, nor did he send in reports for he was a Company Captain. In fact, once near his place we thought we heard a bicycle being pushed in over the hedge, and we were so much in dread of him for we did not want him to know that we were around. He turned up at the Upton Ambush and to my surprise he was given a rifle. He was put in the top gable window of a hut, but just before the fighting started he came down to order a pint and he drank it and then threw his rifle into a coal cellar. The soldiers – I don't know if they were Hamps or Yorks, surrounded the place and they searched the house and they found Coakley who had not fired a shot.[3] Just then the Essex arrived and Percival demanded that the others hand over Coakley, but they refused, for Percival would have shot him on the spot.[4] He had buck teeth, Percival. C[oakley] was then brought in as a prisoner to Bantry and it is

2   Patrick Coakley was captain of Upton Company, 1st (Bandon) Battalion, Cork No. 3 Brigade.
3   The 1st Battalion of the Hampshire Regiment operated from Ballincollig, and the 1st Battalion of the West Yorkshire Regiment from Kinsale.
4   Major Edward Percival, intelligence officer with the 1st Battalion, Essex Regiment, was stationed in Bandon from 1920 to 1922. In 1921 he operated his own mobile column in West Cork to harass the IRA.

said that the Auxiliaries from Glengarriff came in and tortured him. Ten days later I was told by an RIC man in Bandon that C[oakley] had given information. Just about that time two lorries of Auxiliaries lay in ambush and they held up and made prisoners of 6 or 7 lads who were passing by. They questioned them about Connells, but the lads said they knew nothing about the place. Now the woman there had been married twice. There is a little group of houses there, the Forde houses, at [50R] one was the brigade headquarters. Later, when raiding on the evening of Crossbarry they were looking for the old fort out of which the column had suddenly appeared. There is an old fort right enough back there, but the lads had never used it. Then came the round up leading to Crossbarry for the brigade headquarters, but not for the column. It was this round up that led to the ambush of Crossbarry, but not nearly as many British were there as Barry says there were.

Coakley was tried and sentence was to have been promulgated but instead of being sentenced he was transferred to an internment camp. When he came out with the rest of the prisoners he sent word to the battalion that he wanted to meet some of the officers for his conscience was troubling him. He was court-martialled and was sentenced to death, but the sentence being imposed during the Truce meant that he could not be executed, so he was banished for life. In the Cosgrave regime he came back, first went away and then came back again. He lives with a brother and a sister. No one speaks to him, not even the children of the place. He does not go to mass in his parish church, but goes in to Cork. He is a fine looking man, but of course no girl would marry him now. It is a kind of living dead [EOM: *'Poor fellow', I said*].

Tom Barry was a hard man, very strict but very good to his column men, and they loved him. 'Did you have a good billet,' he would say to them next day, 'and were you well fed?'; and if they hadn't been well **[50L]** fed he would move them that night. Always the local company turned out to scout the crossing and to remain on guard, but the column men themselves provided a guard every 2 hours in each of their billets.

Percival: I was captured and I was getting a punching from each soldier as he came past me, and I turned to one officer and I said 'that's a nice thing for a British officer to look on at', for he wasn't hitting me. Whereupon he clenched his teeth in hate and thrust them forward (as if he was going to bite) shaking his head as well with rage. I'll never forget the look of hate on his face.

Tadg [O']Sullivan was captured with an IRB message on him, and he was brought into Bandon (EOM: *Tadg is a brother of Gearóid O'Sullivan Attorney-General*). He was beaten by all the soldiers in the presence of Percival. Then he was ordered to be released, and he was marched down the street with a file of soldiers on either side of him out towards the Hales house. The idea was to shoot him close to the house as a threat. Suddenly Tadg jumped across the road over **[51R]** the ditch and away with him. He was a big burly man, and he never to this day knows how he did it. I saw him the next morning but he was in no mood to talk for he had been lying out all night and his nerves were [not] good. He was a quartermaster and he'd argue with you over a penny. He is a very intelligent man but bitter now.

They came another time to a field when … was working for a Protestant farmer. They jumped in over the ditch on top of him and they were armed with revolvers. Percival was in charge and it was he who asked the questions, and he knew all his movements for the past few days and during that last week. He had left some rifles in the shed of B … a Protestant farmer; but of course C … denied everything. They gave him an awful hammering. Percival said, 'I have my own intelligence service around here and I know everything': and right enough the information was deadly accurate. The raiding party had 2 other prisoners which they put into a forward tender and they put … in the last one which slowed down as if it had engine trouble. There was a side road nearby and when he was being taken down the side road he knew he was going to be shot. He jumped as the NCO fired, and he got away but he was never any good afterwards. When he reported his escape, Hurley, the brigade O/C and … went to B … the farmer. They questioned him particularly as to how the Essex should know that [51L] C was working in the particular field that day and how they could have come on him so suddenly. B … would not give any information and all they got out of him was that at the meetings after the weekly service on Sundays the men remained behind for a chat, and then they would swap stories, or tell what had happened in their neighbourhood during the week in a gossipy way but J ... did not explain how Percival knew that the rifles had been left in J's shed for a night. Next day J ... was gone and we never heard of him again. His farm was confiscated. The minister from Bandon was evidently the local contact and he would be next on the list, so Percival sent word that if he was shot or a hair of his head touched, the P.P., a nephew (or a brother) of the Bishop would be shot.[5] Even then he was in danger for one night he heard sounds in his house and he started up to find men bending over him who were armed with revolvers.

[Jack] Ryan had a running fight with Percival.[6] He came back and reported that he had shot Percival, but Percival was foxing.[7] He had not been wounded, but was waiting for Ryan to come back to finish him off, for Percival had **[52R]** flung himself down face forward on the ground.[8]

Michael Hogan: He was around here in May in the Tan

5   Canon Jeremiah Cohalan, a Bandon parish priest sympathetic to Republicans and brother of Bishop Daniel Cohalan of Cork.
6   Jack Ryan was captain of Ballinspittle Company, Cork No. 3 Brigade.
7   Playing dead.
8   This occurred at an attack on the Royal Marines at the coastguard station on the Old Head of Kinsale on 21 May 1921. Liam Deasy describes the episode in *Towards Ireland Free: The West Cork Brigade in the War of Independence, 1917–21* (Cork: Royal Carbery Books, 1973), pp. 278–280.

War.[9] He was knocking around when Tadg [O']Sullivan, who is very abrupt said what the hell is that fellow doing around here, eating food, let him get off to hell, so I put him on a mule and sent him away, and he went back to Dublin. Then he must have told them in Dublin that he had been in West Cork, but Tadg told his brother Gearóid what had happened and he and Collins made a laugh of Michael Hogan. Hogan was never attached to the column. Tadg was very gruff and abrupt, but very honest. He was brigade quartermaster, and as honest a man as ever saw day light. He would make you account for every penny he gave you or which you spent. Hogan was related to (EOM: *Henry*) Kennedy (EOM: *of the IAOS*) and Kennedy got a job on the White Cross for Hogan, which gave Hogan plenty of money.[10] It was due to a telephone call of Tadg's to Gearóid that old Seán Buckley went up to Dublin and it is a result of that that the negotiations began that led to some kind of a joint army council being thought of.[11] Tadg stood out against Gearóid all the time. He is hard to talk to but he is a good man, but abrupt.

---

9   In June 1921 IRA GHQ sent Dave Reynolds, James Hogan (the University College Cork historian) and his brother Michael Hogan to the Cork No. 3 Brigade for flying column training. Liam Deasy reports that they arrived at the brigade headquarters at an inopportune time and were sent home. See *Towards Ireland Free*, p. 289.

10   IAOS = Irish Agricultural Organisation Society. A former director of the Irish White Cross, Dr Henry Kennedy lectured in mathematics and physics at University College Dublin from 1910 to 1926, and was secretary of the Irish Agricultural Organisation Society from 1926 to 1963.

11   He is referring to the army unification talks in May 1922.

Charlie Hurley showed me a silver ring one day and he asked me was I going to Cork and would I get one like it for him with 3 stones in it. I took it from him but I wasn't able to go to Cork. Leslie Price was then his girl and I handed the ring to ... and told him to give it back to Hurley and when he was killed I asked ... if he could get the ring and give it back **[52L]** to Leslie Price at the funeral and tell her about it, but neither of us did tell her.[12]

What was Charlie Hurley fretting about before he died: was it the failure of the Upton Ambush? At that time Charlie was at his lowest, mentally and physically.

We had 13 companies in the battalion, the 1st Battalion, and it was the best battalion in Ireland outside of Dublin and Cork city. In the Kilbrittain company there were 10 men that Barry could always draw on. At one time reports came in to the battalion headquarters from every company area every day and Kilbrittain company was always busy. Frank Thornton's brother [Hugh] was here as brigade adjutant, but when Michael Collins held a brigade meeting after the camp at G... Thornton was sent out of the area and Liam Deasy became brigade quartermaster. Thornton was accidentally shot in the Civil War as he was coming along in a lorry. It got a severe jolt and a bullet went off and went through his jaw. It was lucky for us that happened for Thornton knew too much about our area.

12   Leslie Price was engaged to Charlie Hurley and subsequently married Tom Barry.

'Buckshot' we called Seán Hales (EOM: *bullshit seems nearer to it judging by Florry's attitude*). Hales would swear and flounder but he was only a lot of noise. Neither of the brothers were fit [53R] to take charge of a brigade or even of a battalion. They were the kind of men the movement threw up earlier and whom it was later found hard to put out of their jobs. (EOM: *They were hurlers or something in the GAA and they, like the Brennans of Clare, they [sic] were fond of themselves and of publicity and decent men at bottom.*) They had made a name for themselves and that name stuck to them.

We had no heart in the C[ivil] W[ar]. Only for Barry and for Seamus Robinson it could have been avoided. They wanted to defeat the arrangement that Deasy and Lynch had proposed for an army unity and it was only because their own names were not on the paper.[13] I said to Liam Deasy the day of the Convention in the Mansion House that they are opposed. I was supposed to represent Tadg [O']Sullivan who could not come up, but the crowd who kept the door in the Mansion House had a photograph of those who had attended the last Convention, so I didn't go in.[14] They'll be 3 armies tonight

13   Begley is referring to the army unity negotiations, which nearly reunited the pro- and anti-Treaty factions of the IRA. Tom Barry and Seamus Robinson opposed a motion to approve the proposed reunification of the IRA during the final army convention held on 18 June 1922. Barry introduced a rival resolution to give the British forces seventy-two hours to evacuate Dublin or face an IRA attack.
14   At this June army convention, a dispute erupted over the admission of non-credentialled delegates. Barry's motion won approval on a first ballot, but was defeated after a screening of properly credentialled delegates.

I said, and sure enough there were 3 armies. Then when the fighting started Deasy and Lynch were arrested and they had to promise not to take action in the south and they were then released.[15]

(EOM: *'That is not true,' I said, 'you must surely have heard Deasy's account of it for you and he are great friends.'*)

'No, somehow I never asked him.' When the attack on the Four Courts was over the fight should have stopped.

Spies: we got word out through the girl here in the post office that 100 rebels had been seen in the hills at Toor; Bantry, Schull and Bandon ba[rracks] had been notified to round **[53L]** them up.[16] At once the word was brought out to the column and Barry moved off through the gap above Dunmanway. Word came that certain houses were being frequented by our men and there was to be an order to raid them. Also there was a name of a man mentioned who used to frequent a certain public house and he was a spy for the British. I was told this

Supporters of Barry's militant motion then left the convention and set up a rival IRA general headquarters inside the Mansion House. Briefly there was the pro-Treaty National Army, militant anti-Treaty IRA inside the Four Courts and a moderate anti-Treaty IRA (primarily from Munster) which established a headquarters in the Clarence Hotel.

15 Liam Lynch, Liam Deasy and Seán Culhane were arrested by the National Army during the attack on the Four Courts in June 1922 as they tried to leave Dublin. However, it was mistakenly believed that as moderates they would not support the militants inside the Four Courts. Under the orders of Richard Mulcahy they were released from custody, though controversy subsequently developed as to whether they had given a definite assurance that they would not join the fighting.

16 Toor is on the Mizen Peninsula.

once when I was in Cork by Florrie O'Donoghue and I was told to move at once.[17] Now, some time before this a girl suddenly came round a corner and she saw a man, who was talking to a police sergeant who was leaning on his bicycle, jump back suddenly over the hedge, but the glimpse was enough for her, for he was the man we were looking for. We captured him and he was shot. Another spy, Lynch, was noticed going around, and we noticed that the people he talked to were bitter and we suspected active enemies of ours in Bandon. One day he came to a lad and he said he had heard there was to be a raid that night and not to sleep at home. The lad passed on the word but the other fellows mentioned in Bandon did not change their houses that night and were captured in the raids. This young [54L] lad did not sleep at home and so escaped. That was enough for us. The spy was court-martialled and was shot. Why did he pass on the word? Maybe to make friends with this young lad for he had being going around with younger Volunteers and had promised them revolvers and he had been anxious to make contacts with young Volunteers.

When Florrie O'Donoghue brought back the 2 children from England, he also brought back a lad from Glasgow who wanted to fight here.[18] He was one of those who went with

17 Florence (Florrie, not Florry as in the original text) O'Donoghue was intelligence officer and adjutant of the Cork No. 1 Brigade (1918–1921) and the 1st Southern Division (1921–1922).
18 Josephine Brown, a clerk in the British Army's Cork headquarters, agreed to provide information to Florrie O'Donoghue if he would kidnap her son

Lordan to hold up a Protestant farmer by pretending they were Auxies[19] and when the farmer saw them he thought they were Auxies and only then by a signal from the Scotsman whose accent would give the others significance did the other IRA understand that they had to play the part of Auxies.[20] 'It's time you came,' the farmer said, 'why didn't you shoot so and so and so and so' mentioning names of active men whom he wanted got rid of. The lads later dressed up, went to visit his brother and he said, 'what a fool my brother was to think that those fellows who visited him were Auxiliaries', and convinced they were Auxies he gave away his information. And he was shot as well.

Reggie, whom she had lost in a custody battle with her in-laws in Wales. O'Donoghue abducted the boy in December 1920, with the assistance of Seán Phelan, the son of Irish immigrants in Liverpool. Phelan then joined the Cork No. 3 Brigade and was killed at the Upton Ambush. Josephine had two sons by her first marriage, and retained custody of the younger one (Gerald) at the time of the kidnapping of Reggie. Florrie O'Donoghue subsequently married Josephine Brown and adopted the two Brown boys.

19 John Lordan was the battalion O/C of the Bandon Battalion at that time.
20 This appears to be a reference to Peter Monaghan, a Scottish soldier of Irish descent who deserted from the British Army and served with the Cork No. 3 Brigade until his death at the Crossbarry Ambush in 1921.

Liam Deasy

(UCDA P17b/86, pp. 6–24)[1]

Liam Deasy (1896–1974) was born in Kilmacsimon Quay, near Bandon and lived his early life in Ballinadee. During the War of Independence he served as the Cork No. 3 Brigade adjutant, and later its commander. At the Truce of July 1921, he was promoted to V/C of the 1st Southern Division, a formation he led in the Civil War. A member of the anti-Treaty IRA Executive and a field general during the conventional fighting, Deasy was perhaps the top IRA leader in Munster besides Liam Lynch. His call for unconditional surrender after his capture in January 1923 demoralised Republicans. Following the Civil War, Deasy helped establish the firm Ideal Weatherproof Ltd, and later became managing director of TrimProof Ltd in Dublin. During the Second

---

1   In this interview O'Malley seemed to summarise Deasy's testimony as well as transcribe it. This leads to frequent grammatical errors and confusion about whose voice is being cited, as does the use of Liam Deasy's name, rather than first person testimony, in many places throughout the interview. Much of what was written appears to be O'Malley's notes on Deasy's insights into the IRB, Munster, and Civil War events. Liam Deasy also made a statement to the BMH – WS 562.

World War he served as a major in the National Army, helping organise the Local Defence Forces. Deasy remained active in Old IRA circles, and after years of work released his memoir, *Towards Ireland Free: The West Cork Brigade in the War of Independence 1917–21*. Its publication generated bitter criticism from Tom Barry, which accelerated just before Deasy's death in 1974. Deasy left an account of his Civil War experiences in his second memoir, *Brother Against Brother*.

Liam Deasy was interviewed by Ernie O'Malley on 27 August 1948 for five hours.

***

[6] Collins saw Seán [O']Hegarty and Florrie [O'Donoghue] the night before he was killed, or were to have met that night.[2]

Seán O'Connell, Col. in Sweep or the Board of Works, was with Collins and Emmet Dalton on the trip.[3]

1920: Saturday after burning of Cork,[4] Florrie and Liam D[easy] came to Dublin, called to arrange for the arms landing, the first one. The arms ship was waiting in Genoa at this time. Florrie then Brigade Adjutant of Cork 1, and he [Deasy] was

---

2   Florrie O'Donoghue, not Florry as in the original text.
3   Seán O'Connell served in Michael Collins' escort during the ambush at Béal na mBláth. Sweep denotes the Irish Hospital Sweepstakes.
4   Cork city centre was set alight by British forces on the night of 11 December 1920 as reprisal for recent attacks by the IRA, causing massive damage to property.

to find a pilot to go to Genoa and bring the boat back. West Cork fixed on but not the landing place, and first met [Michael] Collins, Cathal Brugha and [Liam] Mellows (EOM: *D[irector] P[urchases]*).[5]

Mick Leahy O/C V/C O/C [*sic*] Cork 1 [Brigade] was the [ship] pilot and Moyross Strand at Rabbit Island, inside of it close to the shore.[6] 6,000 rifles and ammo, Glandore Harbour, a sandy bank, to come right in on the strand. No pier, sheltered from the ocean by Rabbit Island, small boats to take stuff off.

Liam Deasy, Brigade Adjutant West Cork (No. 3).[7] Liam Deasy to protect landing and have dumps made locally in case it could not be got through to W[est] Cork. F[lorrie] O'D[onoghue] to take the stuff over at Ballyvourney. We in West Cork to make roughly 100 dumps – which we did. Dumps [were] ready by middle of Feb[ruary 1921] when landing was due. Mick Leahy left on 1st June (EOM: *Now in charge* [7] *of the arrangements of the landing*) for Genoa. At Genoa he found that the British were aware. Word came back

5   At the urging of the Cork brigades, GHQ tried to arrange a large-scale smuggling of Italian rifles into West Cork. Liam Deasy was tasked with organising the landing, while Mick Leahy, vice-commander of the Cork No. 1 Brigade, was dispatched to Genoa, Italy, to arrange the purchase and sea transportation. (He worked with Donal Hales, a resident of Genoa and the brother of Tom and Seán Hales.) However, the plan was aborted after the British appeared to have learned of it.

6   This is at the entrance to Glandore, County Cork. Mick Leahy later commanded the Cork No. 1 Brigade. He was a trained marine engineer with shipping experience.

7   Liam Deasy is shortened to L/D in many cases in the original text of this interview.

from Dublin that Genoa landing was off – (EOM: *The Italians had sold the information to the British. Hales' brother in Genoa knew about the story for I met him in Genoa in 1925/6 when I was on my way to Rome. I had an introduction to him from Monsignor O'Hagan in Rome.*)[8]

Second purchase in Germany. McGuinness and Briscoe [were] over on that.[9] A meeting in Hickeys of Glenville to arrange.[10] Con Moloney, [Seamus] Robinson, Seán Wall, Liam Lynch, Liam Deasy, Florrie [O'Donoghue], perhaps Seán [O'] Hegarty in March. Perhaps George Power, Pax Whelan.[11] (EOM: *George Power, Secretary of the Czecho-Slovac [sic] and Irish Trading Company in Kildare Street.*)

Arrangements of the Helvick Head landing went well into

---

8   Tom and Seán Hales' brother Donal taught in Genoa, Italy and married an Italian woman. He acted as a consul and commercial agent for Dáil Éireann during the War of Independence and helped arrange the proposed rifle purchase from the Italian army. Monsignor John Hagan, rector of the Irish College in Rome, was sympathetic to the Republican cause.

9   Charlie McGuinness (not Maginnis as in the original text) and Bob Briscoe ran guns for the IRA. McGuinness was a self-mythologising sailor, adventurer and IRA activist. A member of the Irish-Jewish community, Briscoe later became a Fianna Fáil TD and lord mayor of Dublin.

10   This was a meeting of Munster IRA leaders held before the formation of the 1st Southern Division, held in Glenville, County Cork during March 1921. The meeting was likely called on their own initiative owing to the failure of GHQ to import arms. It included officers from Tipperary. A second meeting in Kippagh the following month was called by GHQ and resulted in the creation of the 1st Southern Division.

11   George Power commanded the reorganised Cork No. 2 Brigade in 1921 and 1922. Pax Whelan was a senior IRA commander from Waterford.

the Truce. Boat came into Passage in late spring, to Passage East, in Pax Whelan's area. The boat came in unexpectedly.[12]

At end of Dublin conference [December 1920] Collins, we were a couple of days here. Collins said 'were you aware that you nearly had a truce?' Archbishop Clune was trying to make it.[13] Clune saw L[loyd] George, saw Cope on civil side.[14] It was Macready who stopped it.[15] Dublin Castle and the [8] Br[itish] Cabinet agreed, but Macready intervened and asked Cabinet for 3 months to clear up the mess.(EOM: *Did Wilson intervene there?*)[16] Liam Deasy didn't get the impression that Collins was not disappointed at the break.

At Christmas and for 3 weeks later our forces [were] at their lowest ebb.

1921: Collins came to Cork to a Munster meeting of the IRB, September or October [1921]. Liam Deasy, Florrie [O'Donoghue], Liam Lynch there. He said there might be a settlement and must have remarked on something less and Lynch said, 'You'd better not tell them about that when you go inside.'

---

12   In October 1921 the German gun-running vessel *Frieda* landed small arms and sporting rifles at West Helvick, County Waterford.

13   Archbishop Patrick Joseph Clune of Perth, Australia. Originally from Ireland, Clune attempted to secure a ceasefire in late 1920.

14   Andy Cope was assistant under-secretary to the administration in Dublin Castle during the War of Independence from 1920.

15   Lt General Nevil Macready was commander in chief of British forces in Ireland at that time.

16   Field Marshal Sir Henry Wilson was security advisor for the new government of Northern Ireland.

[There was] a violent meeting at Cork a few days after the Treaty [was] signed, before the terms [were announced]. The day the letters were published in Turner's Hotel.[17]

Liam Lynch, [Dan] Breen, Florrie [O'Donoghue], L[iam] Deasy, [Seán O']Hegarty.

Meeting in … Street before debate Liam Lynch, Liam Deasy.[18]

Liam Lynch, Liam Deasy and Collins met before debate at Vaughan's [Hotel]. He said that the 'implication of the Treaty would **[9]** mean a constitution which would be Republican.' That influenced Liam Deasy and they were friendly to Collins. (EOM: *Seán Collins, Mick's brother, has papers in the Land Commission, he was in gaol in Spike [Island] in West [sic] Cork. He may have Batt O'Connor's papers and they are in a bank.*

[Tom] Barry on his own after the Treaty, the Div[ision] had lost touch with him.

Dan Holland in charge West Cork in the end after September when Hales was deported. The best fighting [was] in Bandon, Skibbereen …

Fr Sheehy's book on the IRA.

---

17 This would appear to be 6 December 1921. Turner's Hotel in Cork city then served as the IRA and Truce Liaison headquarters. The 1st Southern Division leadership formally rejected the Anglo-Irish Treaty on 10 December 1921.

18 These are references to the Anglo-Irish Treaty debates held by Dáil Éireann in December 1921 and January 1922. Liam Lynch is denoted in the original text here as L/L and this abbreviation is used frequently in this interview.

– complacency.

– acceptance without thanks.

– wearing out of moral fibre.)

[10R] Dev came as far as Clonmel, and he never came south. I met Dev in Kilmichael the night before Collins was killed, August [2]1st, on a peace mission sounding.[19] Liam Lynch wrote to Liam Deasy letting [telling?] him to have nothing to do with him. He [de Valera] pointed out to Liam Deasy we were beaten out of the barracks, we had made our protest and it was time to surrender. What he had in mind had been fully suggested to Liam Lynch. He also was down, first hand, to hear about the situation. Liam Lynch was hostile.

Prior to Limerick it was with Liam Lynch's consent that I went to (EOM: *Ashford*) train to Newbridge, walked to Kilcullen. Castlecomer – to Mallow.[20] Called [1st Southern] Division together, Brigade O/C and Div[isional] Staff. Florrie and Seán [O']Hegarty disagreed about taking charge and resigned.[21] Florrie then A/G; he had left Dublin after the Convention dispute.[22] I went to Kerry from meeting to

19 Michael Collins was killed at Béal na mBláth on 22 August 1922, so the date of the 1st here cannot be correct. This should read 21st.
20 Deasy refers to the first days of the Civil War just after the attack on the Four Courts, before the Munster Republicans advanced on Limerick city.
21 This seems to have been a meeting of the 1st Southern Division leadership to decide whether or not to join the Civil War. Florrie O'Donoghue and Seán O'Hegarty resigned from the IRA and ultimately led the Neutral IRA.
22 Florrie O'Donoghue was the adjutant-general of the anti-Treaty IRA in May and June 1922, before he resigned. The convention dispute regarded

see [the] position there and there were a few places which I thought would surrender without fighting. Came back to Mallow. E[ast] L[imerick] [Brigade] had occupied house near Ashford in W[est] L[imerick] area. Officer in charge (EOM: *Bill*) Liam Fraher.[23] We had troops from Cork 1 [Brigade] and Lynch [was] slow to start [fighting] with Dinny [O'] Hannigan,[24] and I went down on Liam Lynch's instructions. I met [O']Hannigan and Michael Hogan.[25]

[10L] (EOM: *Liam Fraher: Knows East Limerick, the glen, and Seán Tracey. Lives near Bruff.*

Éamon Rooney: Mayor, Publicity Chief of All Finglas, good man. In charge [of] Drogheda early months of Civil War.)[26]

[11] I think we agreed that we'd withdraw to give them a chance of withdrawing and getting back to their Headquarters with ...[27]

a split within the anti-Treaty IRA over whether to support the Army Unification Agreement, supported by O'Donoghue and other moderates.

23 Elements of the East Limerick Brigade supported the Free State. Bill Fraher, an active veteran of the War of Independence, rose to the rank of colonel in the National Army.

24 Donnchadh O'Hannigan was a general in the National Army and a former East Limerick flying column commander.

25 Colonel Michael Hogan was a close associate of General Michael Brennan of East Clare.

26 The text from 10L, although not in brackets, appears to be notes made by EOM, as the left-hand pages of this interview are generally not used.

27 Lynch negotiated a truce with the pro-Treaty forces occupying Limerick city. During the truce the National Army reinforced Limerick. Once strengthened, Michael Brennan, commander of the Free State forces, ended the truce and attacked IRA positions.

Cork 1 took Adare on way to Limerick.[28] Mick Brennan should have stood by the agreement [with Liam Lynch]. (EOM: *Fraher walked out of Limerick after the Civil War. He was then a Colonel.*) He'd [Fraher] know about the Limerick agreement.

Sandow [was] in charge of [IRA] troops in Limerick.[29]

Liam Deasy, in Mallow, was in [Limerick city] for early fighting for a conference with Lynch.

Sent 3/4 [IRA] columns to Waterford: 1 column to New Ross under [Seán] Moylan, took Duncannon (EOM:?), then on his way to Limerick.[30]

Waterford defended, columns broke up. Hardly any defence made. Only fight was in Kilmallock area, 2 [flying] columns. One in [the] charge [of] Moss Donegan, now in charge [of] Model School, Anglesea [St], Cork.[31]

One in [the] charge [of] Dan Holland, afterwards in charge of Cork 3 Brigade. They broke through [the] line on [the] Bruree side of Kilmallock but [National Army] reinforcements drove them back. They had casualties and captured a good number of prisoners.

28 Forces from the Cork No. 1 Brigade captured Adare and its small National Army garrison in early July 1922.
29 Dan 'Sandow' O'Donovan, a highly active IRA officer from Cork city, was vice-commander of Cork No. 1 Brigade in 1922.
30 Duncannon Fort, Wexford. Seán Moylan was leader of the Newmarket Battalion and later O/C of Cork No. 2 Brigade during the War of Independence. He fought on the Republican side in the Civil War.
31 Deasy is describing the fighting that occurred between the National Army and the IRA in Munster in July and early August 1922.

[12] Liam Lynch:

Clonmel – GHQ

Fermoy – GHQ[32]

Division HQ – Mallow. Early Aug[ust] left.[33]

Bill Fraher told me that when we evacuated Buttevant, Jim Brislane, on 14th August, was captured by Dinny Galvin and Bill Fraher.[34] On 15th he was taken to Mass at Liscarroll and [the] Parish Priest interrupted to compliment the invaders [Free State Army], but Brislane stood up to protest. Galvin put his big hand over Brislane's mouth and said, 'Sit down Jim Brislane and listen to the word of God.'[35] (EOM: [Jim Brislane had been] *arrested at Charleville*.)

[We] blew the bridge in Mallow.[36] [We] evacuated Buttevant and Mallow and returned to Dromcollogher for 2 weeks and sent [the] columns home. [Dromcollogher was] a clearing house for columns from Buttevant and Mallow Barracks.[37]

32 The locations of IRA Chief of Staff Liam Lynch's general headquarters in the first phase of the Irish Civil War.
33 The 1st Southern Division headquarters was in Mallow until the Cork front collapsed after 10 August 1922.
34 Jim Brislane commanded the anti-Treaty Charleville Battalion. Denis 'Dinny' Galvin was a former comrade then serving in the National Army. Commandant General Galvin died in March 1923 following the accidental detonation of a bomb.
35 These two sentences have been inverted from the original for clarity.
36 The famous Mallow Viaduct.
37 These evacuations took place after the National Army advanced into Cork following amphibious landings at Passage West, Youghal and Union Hall on 8 August 1922. Dromcollogher lies in County Limerick near the Cork/Limerick border, close to Charleville.

Kerry Tour after Civil War –

Tan War: Andy Cooney dismissed Paddy Cahill who was headstrong but very honest.[38] He had a column in Kerry, Castlegregory, but gave no time to the brigade and crossed to Killorglin and cooperated with the local battalion or brigade.

(EOM: *Tadg Brosnan was a good man.*)

Andy was O/C Brigade.

Humphrey sent from K[erry] 2 to O/C K[erry] 1.[39] But it didn't ease **[13R]** matters. Cahill had differences with a co[mpany] that 1st fought in Ballymacelligott. (EOM: *Tom McEllistrim TD would know of this as he was the only survivor of the original fighting men. They took Gortatlea* [RIC] *barracks in 1918.[40] Cahill rubbed them the wrong way and this would be one of the causes of the differences.*)

[The] Tralee men remained faithful to Cahill but wouldn't serve GHQ. One battalion under John Joe Sheehy and Con Casey recognised us and the other under P[addy] P[aul] Fitzgerald [served] outside GHQ. In [the] Civil War this battalion remained faithful to the Republic.

---

38   Andy Cooney (not Andie as in the original text), an organiser from GHQ in Dublin, arrived in Castleisland in early January 1921 to reorganise and reinvigorate the Kerry area. Cooney removed inactive and ineffective officers, including Paddy Cahill of Kerry No. 1 Brigade. Cooney replaced Cahill as brigade O/C, but his authority was not recognised by many of Cahill's loyal followers.

39   Humphrey 'Free' Murphy replaced Andy Cooney as O/C of the Kerry No. 1 Brigade in July 1921. He had previously been O/C of Kerry No. 2 Brigade.

40   Gortatlea, not Gortacleagh as in the original text. The attack on this barracks happened in April 1918.

(EOM: *Jimmy Leahy versus Jerry Ryan in Thurles.*)[41]

They got in touch with the Division when [the Civil] war started. Murphy, Sheehy and Cahill there, and Cahill made a plea for unity. Liam Deasy arranged [that] they came in to Kerry 1 as a separate battalion.[42]

[13L] IRB: (13 on Council)

Joe McKelvey on Supreme Council.

Liam Lynch　　　"　　　[representing] Water-ford, Cork, Kerry, Limerick, Tipperary, Clare.

Charlie Daly represented Tyrone, Donegal.

(EOM: *A majority of 4 for Treaty prior to the debate.*)

Florrie [O'Donoghue], County Cork Centre.[43] Liam Lynch with Liam Deasy as his assistant.

Humphrey Murphy – County Centre Kerry? or [Paddy] Cahill.

Pax Whelan – County Centre Waterford.

[A meeting that took place] between Collins's return and the Treaty debate:

Collins president.

Ó Muirthile.

Seán Boylan.

---

41   Jimmy Leahy, O/C of the Mid-Tipperary (No. 2) Brigade, clashed with his subordinate Jerry Ryan, O/C of his 1st (Thurles) Battalion.

42   Cahill's faction had not recognised the Kerry No. 1 Brigade commander's authority. They now formed a new battalion and came under brigade control.

43   'Centre' refers to the individual in charge of an IRB cell.

Martin Conlon? (EOM: *Bulmer Hobson a prisoner in his house*). ... of Hobson.

P. S. O'H[egarty].[44]

[14] IRB – Southern Regional Area before Easter of 1921 for organising the IRB. Meeting of:

Joe McEllis[trim] from Tralee represented [Paddy] Cahill

Dan O'Mahony (EOM: *now dead*) attended

Pax Whelan attended

Liam Lynch   "

1921: After that we put any man of importance in West Cork into the IRB. (EOM: *We felt that Collins would never let us down*.) [We met on a] Saturday evening in Marlborough Street before the Bank Holiday.[45]

1920: Meeting of Brigade O/Cs in August. Mulcahy's plan to let an ambush party fire on us before we fire.[46] Liam Deasy raised the question of an armoured car. Mulcahy took up Macroom, to take it by ... around Macroom ... If they broke through they could be held by the river.

---

44   Seán Boylan was a key Republican in Meath; Martin Conlon of Dublin hosted the kidnapping of IRB leader Bulmer Hobson at the opening of the Easter Rising, to prevent him disrupting the Irish Volunteer mobilisation; P. S. O'Hegarty of Cork (the brother of Seán O'Hegarty), was a journalist and IRB leader, closely associated with London Republican circles.

45   The original text is confusing here, with text crossed out and there is a line that talks about Monday evening but it is unclear what this is related to.

46   Richard Mulcahy was IRA chief of staff throughout the War of Independence. GHQ apparently proposed that the IRA would not fire first on the crown forces without asking for their surrender. This indicates discomfort at the highest level of the IRA with the practice of modern guerrilla warfare.

Mulcahy, Cathal Brugha, Collins, Lynch and Terry
MacSwiney, Liam Deasy, Dan O'Mahony, Kerry 2 [Brigade],
Paddy Cahill, Kerry 1, Earnan O'Malley, Fr Dick McCarthy
represented West Limerick.

RIC Sergeant shot in R[oman] C[atholic] Church in
Bandon. Cathal Brugha [was] very mad. Collins backed him
up. [The sergeant was] meant to be shot on the way to the
church.[47]

[15] D[ick] Mulcahy outlined the development of the war
as General Headquarters saw it … [They wanted] a more open
type of warfare to be developed, and we said we haven't facilities
or arms to do anything except ambush, and I have an idea that
we decided that guerilla warfare was the only solution.

Mick Hogan and Jimmy Hogan [were] with us in West
Cork, Dave Reynolds and a 4th …[48] Tadg [O']Sullivan, Brigade
Quartermaster, who had them for names [*sic*], he sent them
away. 'We have nothing for them to do and we have no food.'
The column had been disbanded, June of 1921. They were to
have been sent back to command columns in Galway.

(EOM: *The idea evidently was to train Mick Hogan and Jimmy*

47 Sergeant William Mulhern, involved in the RIC intelligence department
    in West Cork, was shot dead as he entered St Patrick's church in Bandon.
48 In June 1921 IRA GHQ sent Dave Reynolds, James Hogan (the
    University College Cork historian) and his brother Michael Hogan to
    the Cork No. 3 Brigade for flying column training. Liam Deasy reports
    that they arrived at the brigade headquarters at an inopportune time and
    were sent home. See *Towards Ireland Free: The West Cork Brigade in the War
    of Independence, 1917–21* (Cork: Royal Carbery Books, 1973), p. 289.

Hogan, Dave Reynolds and ... so that they would be able to take over columns in Co. Clare, or in the First Western [Division] area.)

[16] Civil War: Kerry 2 and West Cork (Cork 5) fought best at the end of the Civil War.

Gibbs Ross.

Ted [O]Sullivan (TD)

Moss Donegan

Cork 3 – Dan Holland, John P. Lordan, Florence Begley, Quartermaster Tadg O'Sullivan.

In charge K[erry] 2 – John Joe Rice, Tralee; V/C Con O'Leary.

Kerry 1 – Humphrey Murphy

Kerry 3 – Jer[emiah] O'Riordan.

Kerry 2 – Dave MacCarthy – Portmarnock, a farmer very deaf, perhaps Brigade Quartermaster of Kerry 2.

Dan Mulvihill – Castleisland Adjutant.

West Cork Kilbrittain Ambush June 1919. Successful

Gortatlea, County Kerry. Attack on barracks there March 17 1918, had to retire.[49]

Headford: Dan Allman killed, a very great blow to Kerry as he was the best man, ask McEllistrim who was a very good man.[50]

---

49   This actually took place in April 1918.

50   Dan Allman, not Olman as in the original text, was a senior figure in the Kerry IRA; he was killed in 21 March 1921 at the Headford Junction attack. Tom McEllistrim (not MacEllistrim as in the original text) served throughout the period and later became a Fianna Fáil TD.

[17] Executive Meeting:[51] At Newcastle a resolution handing over power to a Government.[52] [Seán] Moylan, Barry, Liam Deasy, Seán Hyde went back together.

Before going to the Ex[ecutive] Meeting we met Tom Ennis and I think Emmet Dalton and Charlie Russell at Crookstown;[53] Barry had some correspondence with Tom Ennis. Barry and Liam Deasy. Nothing transpired. Fr Duggan had something to do with it.[54]

On our way back we went from Fr Duggan's to the 2nd meeting in Cork city. We saw no purpose in any more of our fellows being killed. (EOM: *Liam Deasy did not take the initiative in going but he was prepared to end the Civil War.*)[55] I was in entire agreement that the Civil War had gone far enough, as I would have agreed with Dev's views in August.

Nothing came out of this second meeting held near Killumney, 6 miles from Cork.[56]

Tom Ennis was there. The meeting [was] prompted by respect for Ennis. Friendly discussions, we were friends. We all

51 'Peace meeting: L/D and' has been crossed out here in the original text.
52 A meeting of the IRA Executive, probably held in late October or November 1922 in Newcastlewest, County Limerick.
53 Major-General Tom Ennis, a top figure in the Dublin Brigade, led Free State forces in Munster during the Civil War; Colonel Charlie Russell founded the Irish Air Corps; Major-General Emmet Dalton was the National Army general officer commanding County Cork.
54 He is talking about peace 'feelers' being sent out.
55 The editors closed the parenthesis at this point, though O'Malley neglected to do so.
56 This meeting appears to have been held on 13 October 1922.

asked is there any way out of it.

Possibly [Charlie] Russell [was] at [this] second meeting.

[18R] In glen for a while.

[I] established Headquarters in Tincurry for 1st and 3rd Divisions in Butlers' and Tobins' [houses]. The Southern Command.[57] I had to see what the situation was in Mid Tipp. I found it contested by Paddy Leahy and a few individuals: no organisation left but a few individuals who were doing their best.

… to Paddy Ryan and from there to Paddy Ryan Lacken's and a meeting of 3rd Southern [Division] held in Powells of … of Ballinaclough (EOM: *1st Dec[ember]*).[58] Seán Gaynor, Lacken and Lehane, Paddy McDonnell, Seán Robins from Offaly and some one from Leix.[59] Gaynor and Paddy Ryan [were] the best. The spirit was good in Paddy Ryan's country and a few were left, but very small in comparison with [the] enemy at Nenagh, and I thought [they were] very little opposition to the Free State troops.

57 This appears to have been in the autumn of 1922. The Butlers' and Tobins' homes were adjacent to each other and located at Tincurry, on the main Cork to Dublin road, about three miles north of Mitchelstown.

58 Deasy is recounting his journey from Cork to the meeting in Tipperary. The Powells (not Pooles as in the original text) were a Protestant family living in the Toomevara district in Tipperary, whom Deasy described as 'very friendly' to the anti-Treaty forces. The 3rd Southern Division (IRA) commanded the following units: Laois Brigade; Offaly No. 1 Brigade; Offaly No. 2 Brigade; and Tipperary No. 1 (North) Brigade.

59 Seán Gaynor was O/C of the 3rd Southern Division; Patrick Ryan (Lacken) was V/C, Tipperary No. 1 Brigade; Seán Lehane was from Cork No. 3 Brigade; Patrick McDonnell (not McDonald as in the original text) commanded the Tipperary No. 1 Brigade during the Civil War; Seán Robins was quartermaster of Offaly No. 2 Brigade. Leix = Laois.

D... of Rearcross: heard of the December executions in a village ... [I] went back to Headquarters, got out of bed. Cross of ... near Oola [County Limerick]. Met Jerry Kiely and Brien in Lattin and got back to Butlers'. We had for 2 weeks [been] attended by Dr John Stokes and Seán Hogan's wife, a form of bad scabies.

Christmas meeting called for Cork and Kerry Brigades at Christmas [*sic*] but I couldn't attend.

[18L] Feeling good in January ...

[19] Seán Lehane came from Donegal to Wexford.[60] Bill Quirke and I left to meet Lehane via Callan [County Kilkenny].[61] Tom Bellows had been sent to take charge of some part of Kilkenny and he was on ahead.[62] We were a day late and on [the] day of [the] meeting at Walsh's, Clogga, Mooncoine [County Kilkenny] [we arrived] to find that the meeting had been surrounded [from] Kilkenny, Wexford and Tipp. Meeting to find out what was ...

Lehane [was] caught on way to the meeting, and the despatch on him betrayed [his] destination of meeting at Walsh's.[63] [My] impression that there was no one [active] in Kilkenny. We crossed to Waterford and back to [the] Nire

60 In the Civil War, Lehane commanded Republican forces in Ulster during the border offensive.
61 Bill Quirke was a prominent officer in the South Tipperary IRA and a member of the IRA Executive in 1923.
62 No information could be found about Tom Bellows.
63 On 8 January 1923, Lehane was captured with Jack Fitzgerald and others in Ferns, County Wexford.

Valley, crossing [the] Suir at Fidown in a currach … and I came back to Tobins'.

Nire Valley's spirit good. [I] stayed in Michael O'Ryan's, a councillor.

[I was] arrested in O'Brien's above Tobins'.

In Clonmel [military barracks after his arrest] don't know what I put in writing for 24 hours. I felt the condition more clearly. Before arrest I felt our chances of winning [the] war were nil. Ned McGrath [was] in charge of the raid [by the National Army] and he was decent. I gave [the] name of Hurley [when arrested].

[20] Within a day or two [I was] tried in Clonmel. Cooney of Carrick [was] present at [my] court-martial.[64] Larry Joy [was] assigned to my defence. Sentence of death. Letter to be given after his death. Letter to Brien, handed to Prov[ost]. (EOM [?]: *Setting out reasons I felt there was no option but to make a move to bring Civil War to an end.*)[65]

Humiliation of surrender: [I] knew I was wrong in taking on a decision which was that of a [headquarters?] staff. Felt he [Deasy] had a responsibility for starting the war, and also for ending it. Same life and I acted accordingly.

Sentence deferred, reprieve at 6.30 in the morning and I didn't expect a reprieve. I felt happy to face death and [a] priest

64 This appears to be Seán Cooney, who had been a battalion officer in the 3rd Tipperary Brigade.
65 This is written as O'Malley's comment, though the voice sounds like Deasy.

came in [the] morning to say Mass and I knew the fellows on the execution squad were more relieved than I was.

[Joe] Guilfoyle brought me to Kilkenny, then Arbour Hill [prison] kept [in] solitary for 5 weeks.[66] I wrote the explanation when in Arbour Hill. Saw Gearóid O'Sullivan, a reference made to the shooting of Collins. He said there were bonfires around when he was killed (EOM: [Michael] *Collins*). They wanted me to give a division [?] but I refused. Seán McMahon and Gearóid took exception to certain paragraphs and I felt I couldn't change and had them relieve myself of any responsibility.[67]

[21] I thought first of Seán Buckley, interviewed him. Then [I] sent out [for] Fr Duggan who took out [prisoners'] letters.

Then [I was] transferred to 'A Wing' [where] Seán Lehane [was] in charge. The wing [was] locked up at a certain hour: we had not the same facility as other wings.

They were looking for a prisoner. We refused to hand him up and we refused to parade.

McGowan [was] in charge of military police and military officers: [the fire] hose got going.[68] Lads – Andy Cooney, Con

66 Joe Guilfoyle was a National Army officer and former member of Michael Collins' 'Squad'.
67 Seán McMahon, not MacMahon as in the original text, was a member of the Volunteers from their inception and fought in the Easter Rising. In March 1918 he became quartermaster general of the IRA, and was a member of the GHQ staff. He went pro-Treaty and was a senior member of the National Army.
68 No information could be found on McGowan.

Casey, Tralee, Stephen O'Neill, Mick O'Neill from Leap, Jack Fitzgerald, Kilbrittain, and Liam Deasy [were] hosed for an hour, then we were dragged on [the] ground down landing to floor and to compound. Compound [*sic*].

Vote taken all over Gaol and there was a majority. Vote taken for the hunger strike. [They] voted in favour of hunger strike. About 10 at end in that wing (EOM: *A Wing*).

22/24 finished [hunger] strike in the two wings. We were transferred to Seán Russell's wing. (EOM: *He was to have gone to Kilmainham but couldn't be found.*

Dick McKee's girl.)

Mick O'Neill: Now [in] Clondalkin married to daughter of Dan Buckley's, a farmer, [he] has great stories **[22]** about Mountjoy – fleas in the cell.

Condemned men brought from Kilmainham. Dan O'Regan owns a hotel in Kildare St[reet, he was] a half chemist at the time. They had a cell with a fireplace, [where] they kept a fire – vermin in blankets. Lehane wrote to Paudeen.[69] Paudeen asked for Lehane, Mick O'Neill and occupants of cell. P[audeen] took out his watch. 'I'll give you 5 minutes by my watch to find vermin.' Lehane wouldn't search. The others searched. No vermin found.

---

69   Patrick 'Paudeen' O'Keeffe (not O'Keefe as in the original text) was a Corkman closely associated with Michael Collins. He was a pro-Treaty TD, the deputy governor of Mountjoy Gaol during the Civil War, and later the secretary-general of the GAA.

(EOM: *Dan O'Donovan from whose house MacEntee began to make the tunnel in to the Joy.*)[70]

'The bones of the goose.'

Fr McMahon: told to leave a cell during the hunger strike, with a boot threatened.

Mick O'Neill

Paddy Mulcahy: Teacher in Balla.

1922 Executive meetings: Early in 1922 Liam Mellows [was] easier to deal with than Rory [O'Connor]. Moylan and Humphrey Murphy signed an agreement.[71] I met Collins and suggested that Dev and Collins get together and suggested that some one whom (EOM: ?) get together when they meet.

Liam [Deasy], Florrie [O'Donoghue], and [Liam] Lynch had difficulty with the **[23]** [IRA] Executive as we did not see Civil War coming and I think our idea was to keep the organisation intact and keep people from going in and that

70   Seán MacEntee, a minister in every Fianna Fáil government from 1932 to 1959, was a trained engineer. Shortly after the surrender of the Four Courts in June 1922, MacEntee and a group of IRA Volunteers known as 'the diggers' began an escape tunnel from a private home on Glengarriff Parade into Mountjoy Gaol. Ultimately, the tunnel was discovered and MacEntee and his men were captured.

71   On 1 May 1922 a group of officers from the pro- and anti-Treaty factions met to try to arrange a compromise that would avoid a war. The group included Dan Breen, Florrie O'Donoghue, Michael Collins, Humphrey Murphy, Richard Mulcahy, Seán Hales, Seán O'Hegarty, Gearóid O'Sullivan, Eoin O'Duffy and Seán Boylan. A document was signed calling for unity on the basis that the majority of people in Ireland accepted the Treaty and that there should be elections to provide a government which would have the confidence of the people.

would keep the organisation intact and that we could influence the Prov[isional] Gov[ernmen]t to break with England.

Were we influenced by Turkey's stand against England and the allies?[72]

Glandore Harbour: The influence of good land around Bandon and areas in West Cork comparable only to South Tipp.

Crossbarry: Movements of [British] troops not as clearly known as Tom Barry points out [in his book, *Guerilla Days in Ireland*]. For the preliminary, British concentration was to find Brigade Headquarters. A prisoner taken at [Upton] station was tortured in Cork and as a result troops began to move in.[73] Barry and Liam [Deasy] did not know of the general [British] advance. They knew only of [an] advance from two directions. (EOM?: *I was there with Barry and Liam Deasy on the ground. We had a much better and a very much different idea of the fight there on the ground as Tom Barry and Deasy gave me information.*)[74]

[24] Liam Deasy's attitude seems to have been determined by a great respect for and trust in Michael Collins, possibly through [the] IRB. Also he felt that the oath and other unnecessary

---

72 The Turkish War of Independence in late 1919 and early 1920 saw the establishment of the independent Republic of Turkey, despite the opposition of Britain and the Allied Powers.

73 The prisoner was Patrick Coakley.

74 Parentheses inserted by the editors. Ernie O'Malley did not participate in the Crossbarry Ambush. This remark indicates that at a later date he visited the battle site in the company of Liam Deasy and Tom Barry.

[Treaty] articles could be changed in the [Free State] Constitution. Always he thought before the Civil War that a strong opposition would stem the swing to imperialism. He did not know of Griffith's influence nor of Kevin O'Higgins's, nor of those who were opposed to Collins.

Even in 1924 Andy McDonnell was approached by Mulcahy to rejoin the IRB.

Liam Deasy's opinion of West Cavan. A very fine crowd of men when he was organising LDF [Land Defence Force] at [the] end of World War II.[75]

The psychology of IRA: taking things for granted.[76]

[Dan] Sandow [O'Donovan] lives in Mallow.

75   Deasy served in the National Army during the Emergency.
76   The text on page 24 seems largely to be Ernie O'Malley summing up Deasy's general attitude, presumably gleaned during the interview process.

Appendix

Letter from Seán Lehane to the Military Service Pensions Board

(UCDA P17b/108, pp. 51–52)

This is Ernie O'Malley's copy of a letter from Seán Lehane to the Military Service Pensions Board, explaining the role played by Munster officers during the 1922 IRA offensive against Northern Ireland, which was recorded in O'Malley's notebooks.

[51R] 'Seán Lehane West Cork (dead)

Office of AAU South Cork,[1]
36 St Patricks Quay,
Cork.
7th March '35.

[To the] Sec[retary],
Military Service Pensions Board,
Dublin.

1   In 1935 Lehane was a captain in the National Army, serving as the South Cork Administrative Officer for the Volunteer Force (a reserve unit of the National Army).

A chara,

The situation in Northern Ireland, during the Truce period in the South, should have a few sentences of explanation from me because it will almost certainly affect myself and those officers who were selected to accompany me to that area, during the early part of 1922. In writing at this stage, I am prompted only by a desire to help your board, and incidentally clear up, or at least help to explain the position of those officers concerned, having learned during the past week that some of them are applying now to establish their pension claims before your board. The difference of their position during the period, forms my main excuse for asking that the members of your board consider my version as follows:

The Truce: While the memorable truce was generally honoured in the South of Ir[eland], it will be recalled that there was no attempt made to recognise a similar situation in the North, and more especially in the present Six Counties, Eastern Donegal and other areas close to the present border. The Crown Forces – Tans, Ulster Special Police etc., whether they were supposed to honour their truce or not still backed up the loyal minority of present Ulster in directing their programme in Belfast and their general reign of terror in **[51L]** amongst the Nationalists elsewhere.

Leaders Conferences: Because of the above situation the General Council of the IRA decided to recognise no truce situation in the North, and ideas were exchanged as to what remedy could be applied to meet the pressure on the Northern Nationalists.

Even after everybody had taken sides on the main question of the Treaty in the early spring of 1922, further conferences were held at which General Liam Lynch RIP and his staff, General Michael Collins RIP and his chief advisors were present, and at one of these meetings the same general attitude was upheld, and in order to remedy things both sides agreed to select officers for Ulster. It was decided that an IRA officer be appointed from the South, and a staff of officers to assist him, that they were to proceed to the present counties of Donegal, Tyrone, Derry and part of Fermanagh and Cavan, and under the direction of the IRA General Council, to assist the present General [Frank] Aiken, Minister for Defence, in war against Crown Forces along the border and further inland in the Six Counties.

I was selected from the Southern Command and sent to take charge of the 1st and 2nd Northern Divisions. Charlie Daly RIP was made Deputy or Vice Divisional **[52R]** O/C. We had with us M. Donegan, Brigade O/C, Jack or Liam Fitzgerald, Kilbrittain, Brigade O/C, Seamus Cotter, Minane Bridge, Brigade O/C. Other officers included Denis Galvin, Bandon, Jim Lane, Clonakilty, Denis O'Leary, Bantry. These were Brigade [*sic*: Brigadiers] and Galvin, I believe Divisional Transport officers [*sic*], also Billy O'Sullivan, Bantry, Divisional Training officer. Tom Mullins, Kinsale, at present in Dublin.

John O'Donovan, of Dunmanway, at present in the USA whose ranks I cannot recall. Others will fill ranks according to facts. I believe I was instructed by General [Liam] Lynch, to take my orders directly from General Aiken. The Truce was not to be recognised up there; to get inside the border wherever, whenever. To force the British general to show his real intention: that was to occupy Ballyshannon, Sligo and along down [that direction].

Both parties – Republican and Free State forces – were to co-operate in giving us arms and supplies, but General Collins insisted on one thing, mainly, that activities were to be in the name of the IRA, and that we were to get arms – rifles – from Cork No. 1 Brigade and that we would return rifles instead to Cork 1 from those rifles handed over by the British. The reason for these stipulations was to avoid embarrassment for General Collins in dealing with the British Government in [52L] case a rifle fell into the hands of the British.

No Truce. We went as ordered and carried out our instructions as far as possible. There were plenty of incidents to show that it was, for the officers canvassed, a period of crowded active hostility, both inside the present border and in lots of cases outside, because the Specials at that time were right, almost, up to Letterkenny. Therefore it was not a period of truce or rest for these men really.

Civil War. Each man concerned will, I expect, fill in his own forms showing the story that continued right along, until civil war intervened. After that a good many Republicans took sides with the National Army and consequently trussed our hands. After their attack on Skibbereen M. Donegan was ordered by General Liam Deasy to remain in the South. The remainder served in Ulster until nearly the end of 1922.

Do chara,

Le méas mór.

Seán Lehane, Capt, AAC,

Div O/C 1st & 2nd Northern Division, 1922.

Chronology of Significant Events in West Cork Related in the Interviews

1919

5 January: Cork Brigade of the Irish Volunteers is divided into three brigade areas: Cork No. 1 Brigade (Cork city and Mid-Cork); Cork No. 2 Brigade (North Cork); and Cork No. 3 Brigade (West Cork).

21 January: Dáil Éireann is established in Dublin.

25 February: Cork No. 3 Brigade attacks RIC barracks in Timoleague and Mount Pleasant.

12–19 August: GHQ training camp for Cork officers in Glandore, County Cork.

17 November: IRA Volunteers raid a Royal Navy motor launch at Bantry pier.

1920

28 March: Attack on Durrus RIC post.

25 April: RIC Sergeant Cornelius Crean and Constable Patrick McGoldrick killed at Ballinspittle.

12 June: RIC Constable Thomas King shot dead at Snave Bridge.

21 June: IRA attack on an RIC bicycle patrol near Bantry, one constable killed.

22 June: Kilbrittain Company seizes Howe's Strand coastguard station.

22 July: Kilbrittain Company again captures Howe's Strand coastguard station.

29 August: Failed ambush at Brinny.

8 September: Ambush of military at Manch, near Ballineen.

4 October: Schull RIC Barracks captured.

9 October: IRA clashes with British Army near Newcestown.

21 October: Two RIC men mortally wounded at Leap.

22 October: Toureen Ambush.

28 November:	Kilmichael Ambush.
28 November:	Mossy Donegan captured.
8 December:	Attempted IRA ambush at Gaggin.

1921

6 January:	Representatives of IRA brigades in Cork, Tipperary, and East Limerick hold a conference in Glanworth, Cork.
24 January:	IRA forces attack crown forces barracks in Bandon.
15 February:	Disastrous IRA ambush at Upton station.
19 March:	Crossbarry Ambush.
30–31 March:	Brigade flying column captures Rosscarbery RIC Barracks.
24 April:	1st Southern Division established.
11 July:	Truce between IRA and crown forces comes into effect.
August:	Éamon de Valera and Richard Mulcahy inspect Cork IRA units.
August:	Cork No. 5 Brigade created from the western part of the Cork No. 3 Brigade.
9 September:	Mass escape of IRA prisoners from the Curragh.
11 October:	Anglo-Irish peace conference begins in London.
16 October:	Mossy Donegan and Paddy Colgan escape from Ballykinlar Internment Camp.
11 November:	IRA lands arms near Helvick Head, County Waterford.
6 December:	Anglo-Irish Treaty signed by Irish plenipotentiaries in London.
8 December:	British government begins to release Republican prisoners.
10 December:	1st Southern Division officers denounce Anglo-Irish Treaty.
11 December:	IRB Supreme Council approves Anglo-Irish Treaty.
14 December:	Dáil begins Treaty debates.

1922

7 January:	Dáil approves the Anglo-Irish Treaty.
7 January:	RIC begins to disband.
12 January:	Prisoners released from British jails.

14 January:	Irish Free State Provisional Government formed.
31 January:	National Army established in Beggar's Bush Barracks, Dublin.
26 March:	IRA holds convention, repudiates the Dáil and sets up an Army Executive.
26 April:	Michael O'Neill, O/C of Bandon Battalion, is killed at Ballygroman, Cork. Thirteen Protestants are killed in the Bandon Valley area in the following days.
May:	Cork and Kerry officers are dispatched to the Northern Ireland border to prepare an IRA offensive.
1 May:	Army unification statement signed by senior IRA and National Army officers.
19 May:	Michael Collins and Éamon de Valera sign an electoral pact to form a unity government after the June general election.
19 May:	IRA begins unsuccessful Ulster campaign to destabilise Northern Ireland.
27 May–4 June:	Battle of Belleek/Pettigo Triangle along the County Fermanagh border between Irish and British/Northern Irish forces.
15 June:	Michael Collins publicly rejects the electoral pact with anti-Treaty Republicans.
16 June:	Irish Free State constitution released.
16 June:	General election returns pro-Treaty majority.
18 June:	Third (final) IRA convention.
28 June:	Attack on Four Courts marks the start of the Civil War.
29 June:	National Army in County Donegal moves against IRA forces.
July:	Cork IRA units participate in fighting in Limerick city, Kilmallock area and North Tipperary.
1 July:	Liam Lynch and the Cork IRA move on National Army forces in Limerick city. A temporary truce is declared in the city.
1–3 July:	IRA attacks and captures National Army garrison at Skibbereen.
12 July:	Temporary truce in Limerick is broken by the National Army led by General Michael Brennan.

19 July:	IRA (including assorted Cork units) evacuates Limerick city.
19–22 July:	National Army captures Waterford city.
26 July:	Cork units involved in intense fighting in Kilmallock and South Tipperary areas.
2 August:	National Army lands in Fenit and captures Tralee.
5 August:	After days of fighting, National Army troops capture Kilmallock.
8 August:	National Army lands simultaneously at Youghal, Passage West and Union Hall in County Cork.
8 August:	IRA evacuates Skibbereen.
10 August:	Republicans evacuate Cork city.
18 August:	Most major towns in County Cork are controlled by the National Army.
22 August:	Michael Collins is killed at Béal na mBláth.
30 August:	IRA attack on National Army in Bantry, Gibbs Ross is killed.
13 October:	Secret meeting between senior National Army and IRA officers near Kilumney.
4 November:	IRA attacks Ballineen and Enniskeane.
2 December:	John 'Jock' McPeake defects to the IRA, bringing the armoured car Sliabh na mBan with him.
8 December:	Government executes Dick Barrett, Rory O'Connor, Liam Mellows and Joe McKelvey.
8 December:	IRA and National Army clash around Kealkil.

1923

8 January:	Seán Lehane and Jack Fitzgerald are arrested.
18 January:	Liam Deasy is captured and issues his surrender appeal.
14 March:	Charlie Daly and three others are executed at Drumboe in Donegal.
10 April:	Liam Lynch shot and dies from his wounds.
30 April:	IRA leadership declares a ceasefire.
24 May:	IRA units ordered to dump arms.
1 June:	Ted O'Sullivan is captured.
13 October:	Republican prisoners begin a mass hunger strike, which ends in failure a month later.

BIBLIOGRAPHY

Primary Sources
Military Archives
Military Service Pension Collection
    Pension and Award Files
    Organisation and Membership Files
Bureau of Military History
    Witness Statements

Newspapers
The Cork Examiner
Irish Independent
The Irish Press
Nenagh Guardian
Southern Star

Secondary Sources
Abbott, Richard, *Police Casualties in Ireland, 1919–1922* (Cork, 2000)

Andrews, C. S., *Dublin Made Me: An Autobiography* (Dublin, 1979)

Augusteijn, Joost, *From Public Defiance to Guerrilla Warfare: The Experience of Ordinary Volunteers in the Irish War of Independence, 1916–1923* (London, 2002)

Barry, Tom, *Guerilla Days in Ireland* (Cork, 2013)

Barry, Tom, *The Reality of the Anglo-Irish War, in West Cork 1920–1921: Refutations, Corrections, and Comments on Liam Deasy's 'Towards Ireland Free'* (Tralee, 1974)

Bielenberg, Andy, 'Exodus: The Emigration of Southern Irish Protestants during the Irish War of Independence and Civil War', *Past and Present*, Vol. 218, Issue 1, 2013, pp. 199–213

Bielenberg, Andy, Borgonovo, John and Donnelly, James, '"Something in the Nature of a Massacre": The Bandon Valley Killings Revisited', *Éire-Ireland*, Vol. 49, Issues 3 & 4, Fall/Winter 2014, pp. 7–59

Borgonovo, John, *The Battle for Cork, July–August 1922* (Cork, 2011)

Borgonovo, John (ed.), *Florence and Josephine O'Donoghue's War of Independence: A Destiny that Shapes Our Ends* (Dublin, 2006)

Boyne, Sean, *Emmet Dalton: Somme Soldier, Irish General, Film Pioneer* (Dublin, 2014)

Carroll, Aideen, *Seán Moylan: Rebel Leader* (Cork, 2010)

Deasy, Liam, *Towards Ireland Free: The West Cork Brigade in the War of Independence, 1917–1921* (Cork, 1973)

Deasy, Liam, *Brother Against Brother* (Cork, 1998)

Doyle, Tom, *The Summer Campaign in Kerry* (Cork, 2010)

English, Richard, *Ernie O'Malley: IRA Intellectual* (Oxford, 1998)

English, Richard, and O'Malley, Cormac (eds), *Prisoners: The Civil War Letters of Ernie O'Malley* (Swords, 1991)

Fitzpatrick, David, *Harry Boland's Irish Revolution* (Cork, 2003)

Harrington, Michael, *The Munster Republic: The Civil War in North Cork* (Cork, 2009)

Hart, Peter, *The IRA and Its Enemies: Violence and Community in Cork, 1916–1923* (Oxford, 1998)

Hart, Peter (ed.), *British Intelligence in Ireland, 1920–21: The Final Reports* (Cork, 2002)

Hart, Peter, *Mick: The Real Michael Collins* (London, 2005)

Hopkinson, Michael, *Green Against Green: The Irish Civil War* (Dublin, 1992)

Hopkinson, Michael, *The Irish War of Independence* (Dublin, 2004)

Kautt, William, *Ambushes and Armour: The Irish Rebellion, 1919–1921* (Dublin, 2010)

Kissane, Bill, *The Politics of the Irish Civil War* (Oxford, 2003)

Lynch, Robert, *The Northern IRA and the Early Years of Partition* (Dublin, 2006)

Lynch, Robert, 'Donegal and the joint-IRA Northern Offensive, 1922', *Irish Historical Studies*, Vol. XXXV, No. 138, 2006, pp. 184–99

MacEoin, Uinseann, *Survivors* (Dublin, 1980)

Maume, Patrick, *The Long Gestation: Irish Nationalist Life, 1891–1918* (Dublin, 1999)

McDermott, Jim, *Northern Divisions: The Old IRA and the Belfast Pogroms, 1920–1922* (Belfast, 2001)

McGarry, Fearghal, *Eoin O'Duffy: A Self-Made Hero* (Oxford, 2005)

Moylan, Seán, *Seán Moylan in His Own Words: His Memoir of the Irish War of Independence* (Cork, 2004)

Neeson, Eoin, *The Civil War in Ireland* (Cork, 1966)

O'Beirne-Ranelagh, John, 'The IRB from the Treaty to 1924', *Irish Historical Studies*, Vol. 20, No. 77, March 1976, pp. 26–39

O'Broin, Leon, *Revolutionary Underground: The Story of the Irish Republican Brotherhood, 1858–1924* (New Jersey, 1976)

O'Callaghan, John, *The Battle for Kilmallock* (Cork, 2011)

O'Donoghue, Florence, *No Other Law* (Dublin, 1986)

Ó Drisceoil, Donal, *Peadar O'Donnell* (Cork, 2001)

Ó Drisceoil, Fachtna, *The Missing Postman: What Really Happened to Larry Griffin?* (Cork, 2011)

Ó Duibhir, Liam, *Donegal & the Civil War: The Untold Story* (Cork, 2011)

Ó Duibhir, Liam, *Prisoners of War: Ballykinlar Internment Camp 1920–1921* (Cork, 2013)

O'Malley, Cormac, and Dolan, Anne, *No Surrender Here! The Civil War Papers of Ernie O'Malley, 1922–1924* (Dublin, 2007)

O'Malley, Cormac, and Horgan, Tim, *The Men Will Talk to Me: Kerry Interviews by Ernie O'Malley* (Cork, 2012)

O'Malley, Cormac, and Keane, Vincent, *The Men Will Talk to Me: Mayo Interviews by Ernie O'Malley* (Cork, 2014)

O'Malley, Cormac, and Ó Comhraí, Cormac, *The Men will Talk to Me: Galway Interviews by Ernie O'Malley* (Cork, 2013)

O'Malley, Ernie, *The Singing Flame* (Dublin, 1978)

O'Malley, Ernie, *On Another Man's Wound* (Dublin, 1979)

Ó Ruairc, Pádraig Óg, *The Battle for Limerick City* (Cork, 2010)

Ryan, Meda, *Tom Barry: IRA Freedom Fighter* (Cork, 2005)

Sheehan, William, *British Voices from the Irish War of Independence, 1918–1921: The Words of British Servicemen Who Were There* (Cork, 2005)

Townshend, Charles, *The British Campaign in Ireland, 1919–1921* (Oxford, 1983)

Townshend, Charles, *The Republic: The Fight for Irish Independence, 1918–1923* (London, 2013)

Ungoed-Thomas, Jasper, *Jasper Wolfe of Skibbereen* (Cork, 2008)

Younger, Calton, *Ireland's Civil War* (London, 1968)

Ward, Margaret, *Unmanageable Revolutionaries: Women and Irish Nationalism* (Dingle, 1983)

Wilson, T. K., *Frontiers of Violence: Conflict and Identity in Ulster and Upper Silesia, 1918–1922* (Oxford, 2011)

INDEX

Fitzpatrick, John James 95, 162
Ford, Patrick 36, 41
Forde, H. F. 48
Four Courts, Dublin 12, 51, 62, 93, 97, 101, 118, 125, 126, 175, 184, 199, 209
Fox, John 117
Fraher, Bill 185–187
Free State Army 27, 56, 125, 129, 187
Frongoch 37–40, 42, 43
Furious Pier 128, 129

G

Gaelic Athletic Association (GAA) 58, 72, 89, 166, 174, 198
Galvin, Denis 83, 84, 87, 187, 204
Gaynor, Seán 194
Genoa 149, 179, 180, 181
Gillman, John St Leger 95, 162
Gill, T. P. 39
Glandore 50, 106, 118, 122, 129, 130, 132, 150, 180, 200, 207
Glanworth 208
Glengarriff 54, 128, 129, 142, 151, 168, 199
Glennon, Tom 84, 85
Glenveigh Castle 86
Golden 53
Gormanstown 116
Gortatlea 188, 192
Gougane Barra 136, 138, 154
Granassig 69
Griffith, Arthur 40, 44, 46, 201
Guilfoyle, Joe 197

H

Hagan, John 181
Hales, Donal 180, 181

Hales, Seán 55, 73, 74, 77, 82, 93, 94, 97, 162, 174, 180, 181, 199
Hales, Tom 48, 61, 72, 82, 99, 117, 180, 181, 183
Hannon, Jim 140, 141, 143
Hare Park 57, 59, 145, 146
Harrington, Michael 130
Hartnett, Noel 160
Hayes, Dick 114
Hayes, Seán 160
Healy Pass 127
Hegarty, Peter 146, 147
Helga 64
Helvick Head 181, 208
Henderson, Leo 50, 51
Hennessy, Jack 54
Hobson, Bulmer 190
Hodnett, John 111
Hogan, James 172, 191, 192
Hogan, Michael 171, 172, 185, 191
Holland, Dan 54, 106, 148, 183, 186, 192
Holmes, Billy 63
Howell, John 106
Howe's Strand 71, 77, 207
Howe's Strand 72
Howlett, Martin 88, 92, 93
Howlett, Mick 65
Howlett, Tom 92, 93
Hughes, Jack 42, 43
Hughes, Patrick 144
Hume, Dick 146
Hunger strike 12, 29, 41, 49, 58, 72, 91, 92, 144, 198, 199, 210
Hurley, Charlie 72, 166, 170, 173
Hurley, Jim 53
Hurley, Vincent 142
Hyde, Seán 102, 103, 105, 193

I

Inishannon 70, 71, 95
Irish Republican Brotherhood
(IRB) 14, 28, 36, 38, 41, 50,
51, 82, 93, 117, 120, 122–124,
126, 148, 169, 178, 182, 189,
190, 200, 201, 208

J

Johnstown 62, 63
Joy, Larry 196

K

Kealkil 60, 67, 133, 137–139,
154, 159, 210
Kearney, Joe 59
Kearney, Pete 54, 59, 103
Keimaneigh 133
Kelleher, Tommy 54
Kelly, Bishop Denis 45
Kelly, Lt Denis 158, 159
Kelly, H. J. 83
Kenmare 112, 127, 160
Kennedy, Denis 163
Kennedy, Henry 172
Kennedy, Raymond 59, 163
Kennedy, Tommy 54, 56
Keogh, Jack 146–148
Keyes, Ralph 24
Kiely, Jerry 195
Kilbrittain 50, 51, 54, 69–75, 77,
83, 89, 95, 98, 173, 192, 198,
204, 207
Kilcoole 126
Kilcoyne, Tom 134
Kilcrohan 128
Kilkenny 11, 53, 85, 94, 113, 114,
147, 195, 197
Killarney 103, 115, 126

Killumney 193
Kilmacalogue 151
Kilmainham Gaol 88, 93, 145,
198
Kilmallock 89, 103, 104, 186,
209, 210
Kilmichael 21–23, 32, 47, 48, 54,
129, 184, 208
Kilmurray 47
Kilumney 210
King's Own Liverpool Regiment
108, 123
King's Own Scottish Borderers
151
King, Thomas 151, 207
Kinsale 70, 73, 82, 123, 125, 138,
167, 171, 204
Kippagh 181

L

Lacey, Denis 'Dinny' 52
Lacken, Paddy Ryan 194
Lambert, Robert 93
Lane, Jack 108
Lane, Jim 83, 134, 204
Lane, Tom 52, 54, 57
Laragh 127
Larkin, Seán 86, 134
Leahy, Jimmy 189
Leahy, Mick 149, 180
Leahy, Paddy 194
Leap 38, 122, 129, 130, 198, 207
Leary, Con 79, 89, 103, 105
Lehane, Seán 30, 47, 48, 60–62,
70, 82–90, 94, 95, 99, 101–
103, 110, 116, 117, 125, 128,
134, 163, 194–198, 202, 210
Lennon, Bill 49
Letterkenny 205